Swimming with Sharks

How to bulletproof your finances for a certain future

(without being eaten alive by the financial services industry)

From the author of 'Shattering the Crystal Ball Myth'

DANIEL BRAMMALL

SWIMMING WITH SHARKS

How to bulletproof your finances for a certain future

(without being eaten alive by the financial services industry)

A guide for the time-poor

Daniel Brammall

This method works in all countries

The framework set out in this book delivers equivalent results regardless of where the reader's country of residence is located, so long as the economy in which the reader is investing operates as a free-market and its jurisdiction is governed by the rule of law. While the reader will need to observe the tax, legal and securities arrangements that apply to the country in which the reader is investing, the universally applicable principles taught in this book operate anywhere in the free world.

ISBN 978-0-6458967-0-1

eBook ISBN: 978-0-6458967-5-6
Paperback ISBN: 978-0-645-8967-6-3

Design and cover art by @aaftabi
Images and Sketches by Edy Salazar
Digital book(s) produced by Booknook.biz

Audiobook, Workbook, And Bonuses

'About 90% of the game is mental . . .
the other half is physical.'

I can't be absolutely sure who said this but whoever you are, I completely agree.

Although what you're about to read is interesting, relevant and exceptionally useful stuff, it would be a terrible waste for it only to be an intellectual exercise. I'd like to think that—at some point—you're going to want to put these ideas into action so you can see first-hand what I'm talking about.

After all, I wrote this book so you could actually **experience for yourself** all of the benefits that this framework delivers.

I invite you to head over to my resources page where you'll find a host of support materials that will help you engage with the concepts you're about to discover. Most of these resources are free and, where a charge is necessary, I can promise you I've worked hard to keep the cost of making them available as low as I possibly can.

Take a look and see for yourself.

www.danielbrammall.com/SWSresources

Listen. It's a tough universe. There's all sorts of people and things trying to do you, kill you, rip you off, everything. If you're going to survive out there, you've really gotta know where your towel is.

—Ford Prefect, *The Hitchhiker's Guide to the Galaxy*

TABLE OF CONTENTS

Introduction

Optimise Your Finances to Bulletproof Your Future

Who this book is for

There's a good chance you're reading these words because you're time-poor and feel disorganised and frustrated about your financial future.

Time-poor because you're good at what you do professionally, yet *frustrated* because your success hasn't carried over to *organised finances*, and a *clear and certain future*.

It's also a reasonable bet that you have a very busy life and —quite frankly—have more than your fair share of other, pressing concerns on your mind. You've probably tried solving this financial planning thing and found it's a deep rabbit hole. You're getting nowhere with it while, at the same time, starting to notice a subtle, growing sense of urgency and anxiety because —let's face it—no one's getting any younger.

Perhaps you've got a financial 'life event' looming—a milestone birthday, a career change, or you've heard a friend's financial horror story and it's reminded you of your own retirement. Navigating that minefield is anything but simple when the economy is the way it is right now, and so-called experts are selling us opposite predictions.

Then, of course, there was the COVID rug that was pulled out from under us.

Remember the shock when there was *no toilet paper* on the shelves for weeks at a time? How about the absurdity of having to wear a facemask in public . . . unless you are holding a cup of coffee?

If we learned nothing else from COVID it was this: you can't take anything for granted. World events no longer happen 'over there, to them'. We are all linked on this spinning globe. Life turns on a dime and a roll of the dice can be felt everywhere, by all of us.

No wonder certainty feels so elusive.

Your task of getting your financial house in order is further complicated by . . .

- *Predators with hidden agendas,*
- *The obligations associated with our daily lives, and*
- *General distractions in this sound-bite, emoti-noise world we live in today.*

Without a compass it's easy to feel lost, drifting directionless in a sea of information, not making any meaningful progress . . . while the clock keeps ticking away.

Someone in this position is perfect fodder for a *fleecing machine* called the *financial services industry,* whose number one job is to fence you in and syphon a little from everything you earn and everything you own.

Don't get me wrong, it's not the people—some of the most-hard working and well-intentioned souls I've ever met work in financial services. It's the industry. It's riddled with *conflicts of interest* and it feeds on your anxiety and fuels your uncertainty.

Because the more complex things seem to you, the more assured it is of its next meal: you.

This book exists to place an independent methodology in your hands which enables you to navigate through that minefield and optimise your financial life so you can get what you want.

Optimising your financial life means you'll be able to withstand the worst economic cyclone, market meltdown or next global crisis. What's more, instead of feeling anxious, uncertain and disorganised about you and your family's future, you have a clear line-of-sight on your progress towards your most important and meaningful goals.

I'm not promising you untold riches and an easy life of outrageous prosperity. What I can promise you, though, is that if you follow the steps in this method, the outcome—as sure as night follows day—*is bulletproof finances and visible, measurable progress towards a clear and certain future.*

Bulletproof, as night follows day.

Bold claim.

"*How,*" you might ask, "*can you promise me clarity and certain progress when you know nothing about me or my personal situation?*"

That's a healthy question, so let's cut to the chase.

The engine that drives this entire methodology is, at its core, incredibly simple yet deeply personal—to you. The framework is fixed, it's the same for everyone. But your content is yours, which makes it personal. You bring your content to bear on a simple navigation tool that puts you back in the driver's seat and takes Lady Luck out of the picture.

We call it *The Independent Planning-for-results Method.*

That's a big promise. So let's get clear on our roles, you and I . . .

In this book I'm your facilitator.

> It's my job to get you results from your time investment here. I'll teach you the Method. I'll show you the ins and outs of each step. I'll coach you a bit here and there so you can take those early wins and keep moving forward towards your bigger projects that have longer-term payoffs. That's my job.

Your role is to own this method, invest yourself into each step.

> The work is yours to do, to be sure, but the results are yours to enjoy, too, provided you follow this simple system. You'll quickly get the answers you seek and start reframing your present. There's a very nice 'double-whammy' to getting your financial house in order, too, which is: you also bulletproof your future.

How to read this book

Your journey through the Independent Planning-for-results (IP4R) Method is broken up into three parts . . .

In Part 1 we'll take a deep-dive into the hurdles that have prevented you from optimising your finances to date, and tease apart real-life examples as lessons along the way. I'll be checking in with you using some self-assessments that point out particular sections of the book I think you'll find very relevant, based on your answers to my questions.

Here's something to bear in mind during this Part: if the penny drops for you, it's totally fine to jump into Part 2 and come back to Part 1 later. Some folks need the meat before they've got the bones, I get that; this book can deliver what you need.

In Part 2 we will unpack the Method itself, exploring how you can optimise your finances using some elegant and proven planning & organising tools. We start to unveil some of the 'assets' of the IP4R Method that will give you a big, big return on your investment of time and energy—your payoff will be in the currency of confidence and certainty.

In Part 3 I'll share how you can start picking the lowest hanging fruit to get those quick wins and build momentum towards a more certain financial future. I walk you through some exercises that demonstrate a particular point, and if you check out the 'Conclusions & Resources' section at the back of the book, you'll find a link to download exercise templates so you can follow along if the mood takes you.

So this is a short book. You're welcome. But let me set your expectations right up front: it might not make sense to conquer all this material in a single sitting.

There are going to be sections of the book you fly through and parts where you'll need more time and space. There are even sections that you'll want to talk to your spouse or significant other about before moving on.

Your journey through this book will be unique to you because of your unique experiences and personality. Pace yourself with that in mind.

Whatever your experience of the pages that lie ahead, I can promise you this: nothing's been held back here, I've 'given you the farm'.

You have *everything* you need to get results because the entire playbook has been opened up to you. If you get bogged down: remember the resources section at the back of the book. Think of it as your 'get out of jail free card'.

Sincerely, I am genuinely excited you're here because The Independent Planning-for-results method is a very simple and effective way to *navigate you through the minefield* called the *financial services industry* so that you, too, can optimise your finances to a bulletproof future.

That's it, my friend. Let's get started.

Part 1

How Bulletproof Finances Means a More Certain Future

How good would it feel—really—if you were rock solid and certain about the future you wanted for you and your family?

You'd have to have visible, tangible proof that you were on track to your goals and your imagined financial future.

More than that . . . you'd need a 'level 10' confidence that your finances were fully organised and bullet-proof, impervious to volatile markets and external events beyond your control.

You'd need to know that if some sort of financial typhoon ripped through the global economy destroying everything in its path, YOUR financial house would still be standing, just as strong as ever, because you built it out of stone.

What would that really feel like?

THAT is the journey we're about to take together . . .

You're ***entitled*** *to these benefits.*
They're yours for the taking . . .

Chapter 1

From 'Disorganised Anxiety' to 'Confident Certainty' . . . and Why This Can Be Your New Reality

The heaviness of uncertainty

You might be used to feeling anxious about the current state of your finances or navigating your financial future. That worry has a weight to it, a feeling of heaviness.

It's not as if you intentionally put that extra weight on your shoulders . . . it just sort of accumulated, one little unanswered question at a time.

You type the question into Google or you ChatGPT it, but you get an answer that raises ten more questions and, before you know it, you're on your way down a bottomless rabbit hole.

So you just get used to living with the uncertainty and worry, continue doing the best you can and keep chipping away at it, squeezing it into the odd evening when you have the strength to say no to Netflix and Facebook. Trouble is, it's still there. Carrying it around with you is heavy, and it soaks into other areas of your life. It's tough to feel light & carefree when the weight of the world is sitting on you.

Here's some good news, though: you don't need to completely solve your problem in order to feel light again.

Sure, solving the problem may well require good measures of your blood, sweat and tears . . . but the truth is that when we catch a glimpse of a solution, we start to feel better already. Your eyes lift to the horizon, your shoulders straighten up, and you breathe again.

That's hope.

The good news is that it only takes a new insight, a shifted perspective, a single 'ah ha' to feel that hope. And when hope is at hand, when you start to believe there is a right track to solving your problem, that feeling of confidence starts to show its head again, those feelings of anxiety lose their grip, you start feeling more certain about your future.

It's just one 'ah ha' away.

A day in the life of this framework

Let me paint you a picture of what life starts to look like as you start executing the Independent Planning-for-results Method . . .

Smart choices based on your bigger picture

Your financial decisions are made based on what's most important to you, your bigger context. It doesn't kill your spontaneity and fun; it just means the strategies you employ are chosen with a clear head and your eyes firmly fixed on the horizon. This means that shiny baubles no longer have the allure they used to have before you could recall your bigger picture. In turn this prevents you from frittering away your high disposable income on meaningless distractions that undermine what you're trying to achieve. We'll start exploring this in Chapter 7.

An end to 3am catastrophising

Another global catastrophe, market meltdown or economic upheaval on the news. You notice your heart didn't skip a beat this time. You realise there are large chunks of the news not worth watching anymore—it's intended to appeal to people who are still adrift in the endless sea of information and speculation. Your focus is now on events within your control. We'll talk about an end to anxiety in Chapter 6.

Clarity and certainty

When you think about those important family objectives you have, they're no longer vague or hazy. That low level of worry in the pit of your stomach when you consider how you're going to make it all happen . . . just isn't there anymore.

What's there instead is a sense of confidence because you have clarity about what the outcome looks like—so much so you can almost taste it—and you know how you're travelling towards it, confirmed by a casual glance at your 'Progress Chart'. You'll learn more about those in Chapter 8.

Direction and visible progress

You have simple, 'everything-in-one-glance' charts to show you your progress. You can see surplus money building up in specific accounts you've earmarked for particular goals—putting money away to help the kids one day, a savings account for a second home, the 'make work optional' account. This is the tangible return on your investment in this process. Part 3 of this book is devoted to how you use this Method to ensure you get the results you're here for.

Financial simplicity

You are simplifying your finances and have a metric that shows you how much more organised you're getting generally, a measure of your overall financial health and well being. This translates to things like having your insurances in proper order, and your estate, wills and trust documents up to date. Having organised finances also means transparency in your arrangements with third parties—no more expensive middle men, silently syphoning a chunk of your hard-won money for valueless services. We'll really unpack what this is all about Chapter 4.

No more FOMO

The painful success stories your brother-in-law spruiks at the family barbeque no longer trigger you because you see them from an entirely different perspective. He's not that clever or not that lucky—he's just lost and attracted to shiny things that someone has repainted a sparkly colour. His financial house more resembles a house of cards, assembled using bad investment ideas and expensive, risky products. We'll 'go deep' on that in Part 2 of this book.

Your support team

Some more good news: no, you don't have to do all this yourself. You have a team of independent experts providing you the support you need. If you're reading this book you're most likely successful at what you do for a living and don't have the time or the inclination to dedicate your few leisure hours to all this stuff. Nor should you, frankly. The last chapter is about building your team.

Experiences like these are common-place among those who have followed the Independent Planning-for-results Method.

The sort of feedback I've heard over the years includes feeling less anxiety, that they're noticing they're not worrying as much as they used to. This translates to better sleep.

Another payoff I've been told about is there's not as much arguing about the finances—in fact, quite the contrary. Partners can actually look forward to talking about their future and their finances together. This means more time and energy and patience handling the kids which, the knock-on effect being that their home life is more peaceful.

Will you experience these benefits? Well I'm not saying that your home life is awful today . . . but what I am saying is that money is a leading cause of marital stress, which can lead to the end of relationships and break-up of the family unit.

Anything that can be done to improve your outlook and reduce friction at home has to be worth investigation, right?

I'm not afraid to say that I have seen the impact on families in financial distress and it's a very significant motivator for me to share this Method with you because that distress is so unnecessary. There is a solution that works.

Tales from the trenches

Sound awesome? Let's confront the elephant in the room . . .

There's no magic wand. There's no fairy dust to instantly materialise results like these. There is a process and it takes attention, effort and time. But the results are real. And they're worth it.

Candidly, as part of the research while I was writing this book, I interrogated the 'before and after' of some of our longer-standing clients who, when we first met, were serious about making the transformation from where they were to the type of reality explained above. What was revealed in this research was the answer to the question: "*What was life like before you implemented this method and what is like now that you are living and breathing it?*"

I've changed their identities, obviously, but their experiences are quoted throughout this book to give you a sense of where these couples were coming from. In all these couples, three stand-out categories emerge:

- The stretched business owners,
- The busy exec/time-poor professional couple, and
- The self-funded retirees.

The experiences of these folks are interspersed through the case studies I'm sharing with you below.

It's important to note that I'm not saying this Method won't work unless you identify with these three categories—we will address what you need for this Method to work best for you in the next chapter. For now, here are three sets of case studies to give you a better picture of some of the key 'before and after' themes that are borne out in the research.

The stretched business owner

These folks are in their late 40s, have kids (pre-teens up to late teens), and are entrepreneurial at heart (or at least one of the couple is!). They own a small but profitable business, turning over perhaps a million or two per annum. They have access to good cashflow within their business so they are accumulating cash but pulling money out triggers a tax hangover the next year.

Self-motivated and ambitious, they work hard but are 'quiet achievers' who go the extra mile for their customers. Although they're not necessarily worried about what 'The Joneses' might think, they are motivated to create an opulent family life (house, car, travel, schools). They are likely to have at least one family pet who they love to bits.

Before

As business owners, Arnold and Grace knew the tax they were paying was significant and they wanted to minimise it. Arnold put it this way:

> *"I don't mind paying my share, but the way the government wastes it is a crime and I don't want to contribute to that. I'd prefer to pay as little tax as possible and instead support causes I believe in, who don't waste the charity they receive."*

Peta and Eric shared this view but, as their children were younger, they were also worried about whether they had enough insurance. They didn't feel they could approach an insurance agent because:

> *"It's like asking a barber if you need a haircut."*

Both couples shared the desire to give their kids the best possible start they could afford to give them.

They voiced their concerns and ideas to their accountant, who was enthusiastic to help, but they didn't really get a sense of direction from the ad hoc solutions their accountant was volunteering. Also, the solutions presented to them seemed to create more complexity rather than simplicity.

In frustration, Arnold took matters into his own hands and did a course on share trading, and Grace crossed her fingers. Together, they started researching venture capital and became an angel investor to a start-up business.

Executing the IP4R Method

Embracing the concepts that we'll explore in Chapter 4,

they used a tool called the 'Report Card' (Chapter 11) to get a clear picture of what was 'broken' and needed fixing first, and what could be left alone for later. Arnold and Grace likewise took stock but, being at a different stage in their lives to Peta and Eric, prioritised other projects to get organised.

This included a wealth planning exercise to work out just what their businesses needed to be worth at various points in the future, to fund their retirement goals. A meeting was called with some of their other advisers, notably their accountant and lawyer, to hold a 'Strategy Brainstorm' (Chapter 12). This enabled them to develop ideas on restructuring their businesses to minimise tax and ensure a clean exit, when that time comes.

It also meant having a funding blueprint for their retirement plans, insurances, and cashflow plans for their other goals, a process we unpack in Part 2 of this book.

After

They've been able to realise their dream of helping both their adult children into their first home. Grace was able to make the decision to quit her high paying job in child protection and pursue her calling to work for a charity that finds homes for children in need. Arnold completed his first Ultra Marathon in Japan. He still manages a share portfolio, but it's for fun rather than the main pillar of his retirement strategy.

Peta and Eric unfortunately lost the money they invested into the start-up, which hurt . . . a lot. They regrouped, though, and shifted their focus from being all-work-no-play to 'what are we doing all this for?'. In time, they bought a holiday house on the coast which they rent out through Airbnb when they're not using it. They're renovating the family home (again). Emma's also taken up quilting and sewing and is now making the kids all their clothes.

The busy exec/time-poor professional couple

This couple is well educated, 50-something executives (high-level public servant or 'C-suite execs' in private enterprise) or professionals (doctors or medical specialists, senior lawyers or barristers). As a couple, they are earning between $500k and $1m a year and have children who are still living at home.

Although they want a lifestyle today, they are also highly focussed on their financial future.

Their hobbies are modest/simple; they like to travel, they value family, and want to give their kids a leg-up when they reach their twenties so they get the best start they can in an unforgiving world. These couples value their time and they value expertise—they are 'delegators' who prefer a relationship with someone they trust because they don't have the skills, qualifications, experience, time or connections to the best job themselves of getting their finances on track. This would free them up to pursue more important projects.

They generally have a reasonable emotional IQ ('EQ') and might have a tendency to anxiety if they feel vulnerable, exposed, or disorganised/not fulfilling their family values and delivering the best they're capable of for their families. They don't want to be misled or beholden to anyone and are looking for someone they can trust.

From this perspective, it's easy to see how these qualities of desire-to-delegate and prone-to-anxiety can cause all sorts of friction.

Before

Edward and Cassie explained to me that their number one problem was no real clarity and therefore no real progress. Cassie put it this way:

"We don't know what we don't know."

They hold very demanding roles professionally and felt they didn't have the time or expertise (or interest, frankly) to do the best job possible. All their attempts at solving this exhausting dilemma had so far resulted in no appreciable progress.

Gwen and Lyle felt the same way. Both medical specialists who work long hours and are often 'on-call', they explained to me that their days seem to be a constant juggle. Their number one goal was to be free to concentrate on their professions without 'getting it wrong' weighing on their minds.

Executing the IP4R Method

Gwen and Lyle's first priority was to establish a team to hand off all the management of their finances and a lot of the worry with it; they basically became the 'poster child' of Chapter 13.

By contrast, Ed and Cass really invested themselves in clarifying their bigger picture and establishing what 'must-haves' they needed to have in their lives, concepts you'll learn about in Chapter 8. This made it easier for them to let go of the roadmap a little, without letting go of the steering wheel.

After

Ed is very successful in his career. In his particular field, he's responsible for decisions whose ripples are felt by 80,000 staff nationally. Ed loves the progress tracking tools that are part of the heart of this Method. Watching him soak up the simple progress charting processes from the relaxed position of spectator on the couch must be a nice break from the gravity of his professional role.

Gwen and Lyle report feeling much more organised, like someone's got their back, nothing's being missed and nothing's left to chance. They still work crazy hours but they've never missed a progress meeting. An observation from one of my staff:

> *"Yes, they earn a million dollars a year between them, but they still really prioritise it, they hand it all over . . . and they're doing really well as a result of it. It's so good to see. They're wonderful."*

The self-funded retiree

These folks were once successful execs, professionals and/or business owners during their working lives and have self-funded a reasonable retirement. Importantly, they're down-to-earth folks who don't see themselves as rich—a millionaire isn't what it used to be. They've just accumulated funds over their lifetimes and won't get another opportunity to do that if they make a mistake now.

Their children are all grown up and close to them. They have strong family values, and their adult children possess these same qualities, a source of pride for our self-funded retiree. They want to see their children be successful in their chosen careers and would like to see them become similarly successful parents.

Having achieved much in their careers they have developed wisdom and scepticism/cynicism in no short supply and have the battle scars to prove it. While they are not necessarily price sensitive, they are certainly not going to be 'taken for a ride', they know the value of a dollar and they have developed a keen 'BS alarm'.

Financially they believe this is their last shot—they don't get a second chance to earn all their money again so they don't want to blow it chasing rainbows. They want certainty about the security and performance of their money and believe in chasing talent and getting good value.

Although they're not disloyal, they probably have been sufficiently burnt during their working lives and aren't blindly loyal. They believe people should be judged on their merits and are prepared to give someone a fighting chance to prove themselves but not by putting themselves in jeopardy. This has something to do with the gravity of their position inasmuch as they don't have the chance to earn this money again if they blow it, and they didn't get to where they are in life by being reckless or naïve.

Before

In these couples the task of managing the money seemed to naturally fall to one of them. Generally this individual had the 'busier personality' of the two of them and, also being gifted with a strong intellect, soon fell prey to 'The Complexity Habit' that you'll read about in Chapter 2.

Cutting through the complexity, though, their number one problem, as stated, was making their accumulated wealth last for life. As Tony so concisely put it:

> *"We don't get a second chance at this . . . I don't want to have to earn it again."*

With this in mind, it made sense how important it was for them to get it right. Strangely, both Tony and Dorothy and Lisa and Jeremy already had a financial adviser, but there was something not quite right. Each time they visited their adviser, they came away feeling punch-drunk with numbers, like the adviser's job was to love them to death with complexity. However this was counter-productive; what was missing for each couple was a sense of certainty and confidence.

Executing the IP4R Method

It was love at first sight for Lisa and Jeremy when they met the 'Safety Review' exercise you'll read about in Part 3. This process really turned the light on for Lisa in particular, and she could relax from 'white-knuckling the steering wheel'.

> *"I felt like—oh, I can relax and trust this. Everything's going to be okay."*
>
> **—Lisa H**

For Tony and Dorothy the features of this Method that bring them the most comfort is its transparency. Transparency resonated particularly with Tony who operated a successful franchise business for many years and knows only too well how hidden agendas can undermine any objective, no matter how worthwhile.

> *"Lazy middle-men, man . . . toxic, I tell you."*
>
> **—Tony R**

After

Tony and Dorothy spend more time touring on Tony's motorbike and camping with their adult children and their spouses than they ever did when they were managing all this complexity themselves. During their middle years, Tony was the breadwinner and Dorothy the homemaker, and Tony seemed to fall into the job of managing their finances. Although Dorothy felt he was doing a great job, at least as far as she was concerned, for many years she was worried that life was slipping by and Tony was missing out.

I sense they've been relieved of a long-standing tension between them. They now teach other couples how to reconnect with each other and work better as a family unit. I love spending time with this couple.

Jeremy, now in his late 60s, is in superb shape and carving up the ski slopes. Jeremy and Lisa came back not that long ago from a skiing holiday in Japan with their 4 adult children, their spouses, and all the grandchildren. The deal was Lisa and Jeremy would pay for the month's accommodation if their kids and their family made their own way there. (I made a mental note to implement the same idea one day.)

The simple regular tracking program means they no longer have to spend whatever time they have left on the planet mastering all the complexity of their finances. They can check in at pre-set periods to make sure things are still on track and, if they're not, work out what needs to be done to get back on track, then get back out on the ski slopes.

Another couple, Danny and Leigh, now that they are unburdened of money anxiety, have made it their mission to make the most of this 'gift of time'. Although Danny's knees finally gave up the ghost and he had to give up professional dancing, he's got a new lease on life now that he's sitting on the board of a not-for-profit that sponsors and supports young talent in the Arts sector. Leigh's new hobby is planning trips to somewhere on the planet that they haven't experienced yet.

As you can see, adopting this Method can have a far-reaching, positive impact on your life.

What if these people aren't me, though?

Here's some reassuring news for you: you don't need to be any of those people to get the results of this Method. I simply chose those examples because they are amply represented in the body of work we've done—we have clear evidence that the process works and a couple of clear demographic categories have revealed themselves in those folks who are clients of ours, most of them for over a decade now.

You might be in construction, retail, the public service, the military. You might be a consultant, a contractor, or someone who retired long ago. Provided you have your eyes on the horizon, then this method can work for you.

In the many years of doing this, I've found this method will work for anyone provided they have these two essential ingredients . . .

The first of those is that you need an *economic engine*.

> If your economic engine peters out and you're forced to live on social security, then there's some work you need to do before you're ready to start. That's beyond the scope of this book.

The second essential ingredient you need to make this work for is a *desired future*.

> If you have run out of aspirations and aren't really motivated to carve out a future by design, then go do whatever takes you fancy because this Method exists to create certain results, on purpose.

We'll dive a little deeper into what you need to make this Method work for you in Part 2 of this book. For now, though, considering the above, there might be another question on your lips: "H*ow long do I continue using the Independent Planning-for-results Method?*"

The answer is "*for as long as you have an economic engine and a desired future.*"

Direct your economic engine towards your desired future

What you're going to read in the pages ahead is not actually a solution built to achieve more stable returns, contained risks, reduced costs and taxes. Those are side-benefits.

Also, while this framework is a solution that optimises all your finances, that's just the process.

The Method laid out in the pages ahead delivers more than these two benefits. It's actually a methodology for directing your economic engine towards your desired financial future so that you can create the life you want for you and your family, by design.

Let's get started.

Ah ha's . . .

- *Uncertainty and anxiety about your finances and the future are a leading cause in disagreements and disharmony between couples and can erode the family fabric.*
- *Moving from a place of uncertainty and anxiety to a clear sense of direction and confidence is available to anyone with an economic engine and a desired future.*
- *Replacing the feeling of financial uncertainty and worry with a growing sense of clarity and optimism is achieved by a single step in the right direction. Take that step.*

Chapter 2

Scratching Your Itch

Ever had that experience where you were struggling with a problem, and even though you'd worked out 'the name for your pain', in spite of the best efforts of you and everyone helping you, it wasn't quite scratching that itch?

Here are three couples having that same experience. I share these with you not because they're mind-shattering rags-to-riches success transformations, but because each couple's story exposes the problem beneath their problem.

Plus, if you see yourself in any of these examples, I want you to know this book is for you.

Drawn from the research on the three stand-out categories from last chapter, these case studies give you the viewpoint of the proverbial fly on the wall. Perhaps some of what you're about to read might start to sound familiar . . .

Back to the busy exec/time-poor professional couple

Justin's a sharp guy. He's a contracting engineer in his late 40s, married to Jane, who's also pretty sharp and has worked her way up through the ranks and is now high up in the military.

Together they have three beautiful boys under eight, a lovely home that's mostly paid off, and about a million dollars in the bank—the proceeds from some property successes from a few years back and a small 'side hustle' Justin got into when taking a break from the grind of big contracts that they got out of last year.

Now back in full swing at work, they earn well over half a

million dollars a year between them from their very demanding professions. Together they have survived several adversity events, personally and professionally and have picked themselves back up and worked as a team to get themselves into this position. Justin and Jane know the value of hard work, of focus, and of taking responsibility for getting the job done. They, as you'd expect, don't have a lot of time to muck around and certainly don't suffer fools gladly.

When they came to see me, Justin led from the front. He knew what the problem was, had researched the technical aspects to investment analysis, had worked out the three highest options, and wanted to explore them *ad nauseam*.

Jane's view was that he wasn't wrong, but he wasn't entirely right either. She was convinced that they could keep this pace up for maybe another ten to fifteen years, and that the state of the economy was at a something-o'clock right now, which meant they had to take a particular course of action now because they're not going to get another shot at this.

The Complexity Habit

Sometimes, when faced with a big problem, we think we need a big, complex solution.

It's counterintuitive to relax a tight grip when the stakes are high, but just ask any professional sportsperson how valuable this tip is. It's not easy to do, though, when letting go means falling into a pit of alligators.

So Justin and Jane's first task was to pull back from all the details of the problem to a 50,000-foot view. Being able to see your bigger picture in this way immediately relaxes your grip because you don't have to hold on to everything; you can see it unfolding in front of you, everything in view.

I'll show you how to do that in future chapters but for now, just put that one into your memory bank. It will be needed later so you can look at your situation from a bigger perspective, like Justin and Jane.

Remember the stretched business owner?

Pete and Jillian are in their 50s and their kids are growing up. They work hard but they're also starting to enjoy the fruits of their labour. The business they own turns over a bit over $2m a year now. Their staff seem to know how to do their jobs now and don't need to be managed 24/7. Usually.

Peter and Jillian have taken risks, made mistakes, and have the scars to prove it. But they're okay. They're tight as a couple, the kids are shaping up nicely, and they're starting to show signs of pulling some of that profit out for things they can enjoy, like the holiday house at the coast, the extension they're planning for their home, and their growing 'overseas holidays' budget.

Pete started taking antidepressants six months ago.

This happened after a health scare that the doc told him was actually stress-related. It wasn't a heart attack or anything as dramatic as that, just a kind of weird episode one evening that shook him up. It was as much a surprise to Peter as it was to Jillian. They both thought he was coping just fine.

Peter's no slouch. A few years after the birth of their second child, he noticed he was getting a bit soggy around the mid-section, so he got fit. He didn't just get fit, he ran a marathon.

And as for Jillian, to describe her as capable is an understatement. You don't need to be in a conversation with her for long before you realise that she's well and truly awake at the wheel and means business. These guys are remarkable copers, and as a team, they're an admirable powerhouse.

Nevertheless, their two investment properties and self-managed share portfolio are reactions to a feeling that is not going away. They're headed forward at a million miles an hour but they're no closer to knowing whether the way they're going is the right direction, and this 'silent anxiety' is gnawing away at their peace of mind, to say nothing of the time and energy it's costing them—both in short supply. The cracks are starting to show and, if their family doctor is right, left unattended, these cracks will grow.

The Magic Pill Culture

We live in a magic pill culture. Take this pill, it cures your headache. This means you don't need to let the headache occupy any more of your valuable time and your attention can return to bigger, more pressing matters. It's a sign of the times, you see—the sheer pace we need to live our lives at means moments of deep reflection on the bigger picture are elusive, at best.

You see evidence of this when you play 'connect the dots' with Pete and Jill's investment portfolio. When you connect the dots you should be able to see a picture of what that collection of dots is supposed to be. If, when you connect all the dots, where there should be a picture all you can see is a scribble . . . it's a pretty good sign that there was no rhyme nor reason for the dots in the first place.

The investments were Pete and Jill's dots, the portfolio an expensive scribble. This became painfully clear for this formidable couple when they drew their finished picture and realised that connecting their dots doesn't look anything like the picture they wanted. I'll guide you through this process later in the framework.

The 'self-funded retiree' experience

Bernie's business was worth a bit over $5m on paper when I met him. He told me he felt uneasy—not quite burnt out but certainly jaded—and now that he was knocking on the door of that magical 60th birthday, he and Grace had talked about him getting out.

He was worried whether it was enough to last the rest of his life so he soldiered on. When he sold the business a few years later, it was worth a couple of million more. Surely that had to be enough.

He'd actually been seeing a financial adviser for a few years already when he came to me for a second opinion. He felt troubled by a lack of reassurance from the detailed product reports that he received each quarter. Full of appealing graphs and sage reasons why each investment had earned its place in his portfolio, Bernie was still buried deep in research, drilling his way to the centre of the Earth, trying to get to the bottom of why he couldn't shake this background anxiety.

As far as Bernie was concerned, the problem was obvious—the returns from his portfolio weren't good enough. The economy goes up and it goes down, it cycles. He reasoned:

> *"Surely if you've got the connections and you're 'in the business', you are plugged into all that stuff."*

On this basis, he was quite right to be asking the question why there were other investments out there that were doing better, why he didn't own them. Or at the very least, when the economic cycle hits 'whatever o'clock', he was expecting a phone advising him to pull out so he didn't walk off the cliff.

I asked Bernie what return his plan needed to deliver him so that he could be confident his wealth would last forever. The answer I got took me on a tour of the economy, of market behaviour, of what his stockbroker charges, how everything's so expensive and unpredictable, and in the end he had to ask me what the question was again.

He was obviously frustrated. It was also obvious he had no clarity about his problem, much less a solution: it was a very simple question and he had no answer for it.

Forest and Trees Syndrome

Bernie had lost sight of the forest, all he could see was trees. Whereas Bernie was looking outside for a culprit, he needed to look closer to home. Ironically, Grace had no problem seeing the forest—she was able to keep clear sight on the context of her life and didn't get so caught up in the content.

Sure, Grace told me how grateful she was for Bernie's hard work and success, and she had always trusted his judgement in these matters. Don't be fooled by appearances, though, Grace was no absent landlord . . . when they told me their story over the last four decades or more and how they'd come to be where they were, it was abundantly clear that Grace had been Bernie's rock through good times and bad.

Make no mistake, that's rare. And exceptionally valuable, especially if you're put together like Bernie is.

The light went on for Bernie when he was able to see that each of the minute details in his finances was part of something bigger, and that these larger pieces of the puzzle connected together to form a bigger picture.

The concept that worked for him was looking at all the disparate minutiae of his finances as mere pieces of furniture in the various rooms of his 'Financial House'. The furniture can be moved around to open up the room's space and have it function in a different way. It can even be replaced if it doesn't serve the purpose of the room. Or the room can be repurposed to better serve the layout of the whole house. We'll explore this idea of your Financial House repeatedly throughout the course of this book.

Chasing your tail

As you can see from the examples above, we're all under stress. We're all time-poor. We're all getting it from every direction. It's no wonder we're all out chasing solutions to problems, answers to questions. Why do you think the interwebs is such a huge hit?

How do I get higher returns, reduced fees, better investments, more comprehensive insurance, reduce my tax, make my retirement nest egg last for life?

We're out chasing an answer because we think that will be the solution to our problem.

The Complexity Habit, The Magic Pill Culture and Forest and Trees Syndrome . . . these are symptoms of this lifestyle, this approach to problem-solving. They treat the symptom, not the cause, which is the reason you don't feel better, the reason you still feel uncertain and anxious. It's why you don't have any evidence you're making clear progress towards your desired destination.

The answer that cuts through this problem all lies in your framework. It worked for the couples above, and it can work for you and your family's financial future.

Success Check-in exercise

The Complexity Habit, The Magic Pill Culture and The Forest and Trees Syndrome are examples of what can prevent you from making real progress towards financial certainty and confidence. Before you start to walk through the framework, let's first check in with where you're at right now in terms of your openness to embrace the new ideas and thinking in this book.

Below, rate yourself on a scale from 1–5 on how accurate the statements are—1 means 'not accurate at all', and 5 means 'most accurate'.

Once you've rated yourself for each statement, total up your scores and then use the Answer Key to determine your next steps.

	Statement	Score
1.	When it comes to planning my finances I feel stuck/caught in a loop.	___
2.	I fear I may be researching my way to an early grave.	___
3.	Being beholden to someone else for a solution is starting to look inevitable.	___
4	I have no idea how my finances would stand up in the event of a catastrophe.	___
5.	I lose sleep over my future finances.	___
6.	My spouse and I don't see eye to eye on how to arrange our finances.	___
7.	My finances feel disorderly.	___
8.	I'm used to a low level of anxiety about financial planning that's always with me.	___
9.	When I think about the state of my financial affairs, I don't feel confident.	___
10.	My spouse and I don't have a clear direction in our financial planning.	___

11. The more I look into areas of finance, the more complexity I discover. ____________
12. My options don't appear to be clear to me. ____________
13. I don't feel in charge of my finances, I feel constrained by them. ____________
14. I got advice previously, however it hasn't dispelled these feelings of dissatisfaction. ____________
15. I am in an advice/investment program that isn't very satisfying. ____________
16. My experience with advisors is the solutions are more complicated than the problems. ____________

Total Score ____________

What Your Score Really Means

Score: 0 – 24

Get ready to soar

You're going to enjoy the new thinking and ideas in this book. All you need to do is follow the Method you're about to learn and you'll be well on your way to having a clear financial future and feeling very organised about your finances.

You're probably going to be tempted to skip ahead from time to time. Nothing wrong with that for you, but make a note to return to the skipped sections later so you can 'backfill' any missing concepts. That way you'll get the most from what this framework has to offer you.

You're probably going to love the thinking behind '**Expecting the Unexpected**, which is going to be covered in Part 3 of this book.

Score: 25 – 59

The Heartland

If you landed here, it means your past experiences are probably holding you back at least somewhat, and many people have this in common when trying to plan their financial future. There's a little work here for you to do to get up to speed, but if you can stay with the new ideas and get your head around the concepts as they're explained in this book, it's going to make life much easier for you. You should be able to implement the method efficiently and effectively.

My advice to you as you read through this book is to pay particular attention to a concept you'll hear repeatedly: your *'Must-Haves'*. Being clear on this may well be a big 'ah ha' for you.

Score: 60+

Your peace of mind is on the line

It's been quite some time since you had a sense of confidence and simplicity about your finances, and it's starting to cost you personally. Take solace: you're not alone! I'm probably not telling you anything you don't already feel very keenly: a solution that actually works is long overdue. On the bright side, you stand to benefit the most from implementing this framework, because the results you experience will be so transformative for you.

Here's how I suggest you proceed as you work your way through the methodology in this book: pay particular attention to Chapter 4. A light should go on for you . . . *that chapter was basically written for you*. You may well find the concepts in Chapter 6 will bring welcome relief, too. Don't skip ahead—there is some groundwork that must be prepared before you're going to be ready for the ideas in those chapters.

Chapter 3

Overcoming Hurdles, Removing Roadblocks

In the middle of the night
I go walking in my sleep
Through the jungle of doubt
To a river so deep.

—**Billy Joel,** *River of Dreams*

The jungle of doubt

That wonderful lyricist, Billy Joel, spoke to each of us in his song, *River of Dreams*, when he described what was keeping him awake at night: doubt, frustration, anxiety, uncertainty.

These exhausting emotions are symptoms of the roadblocks we unearthed last chapter: the Magic Pill Culture, the Forest and Trees Syndrome and the Complexity Habit. Often these slumbering ogres are stirred awake by a triggering event or life situation, like . . .

- A milestone birthday—your 40th, 50th or 60th—that brings with it a growing sense of dissatisfaction that something in your life is lacking that would likely be solved by money.
- A slow realisation that you have no idea when work will become optional financially, or even whether it will at all.
- A short, sharp pang of panic when you hear a friend's horror story and become aware you're exposed financially and the same could happen to you.
- A secret and resentful pang of FOMO as you read a 'financial windfall' story online (of course, the story neatly side-steps all the risks that were involved plus the

sleepless nights full of worry about the strategy failing and toppling their finances like a house of cards).

One of these events may have woken the beast. In response you took up arms and did something about it, but it didn't bring you lasting peace, the ogre still roams, its roars echoing through the hills and keeping you awake at night. The only way to vanquish this pest for good is to properly understand your foe.

So let's dig deeper.

The Complexity Habit

Last chapter, you heard the story of how some 40- or 50-something professional couples and executives had become bogged down by this problem. This happens because it's served them well in the past. It's how they make their living.

For example, in the case of a couple who is a member of the professions, they spend their days prescribing solutions they spent years and years and years studying. The biggest thorn in their side is the client or patient is unlikely to follow the advice unless they understand it . . . but the client/patient doesn't even have the vocabulary to participate in that conversation.

Similarly for the busy executive whose direct report comes to the exec with a problem and it soon becomes apparent the report is describing the symptoms of an underlying problem which is, frankly, beyond the report to grasp. The only solution here is to get involved, head up the research team and take everyone involved on a journey.

The two scenarios presented above don't present a dilemma professionally because this is how our couples make their living. They have the time and the money, it's what they're trained to do, and so they execute on that training to get the result and everyone moves forward.

If that sounds like you, it's entirely possible that you've developed 'the Complexity Habit' and it's not going to serve you once you meet the financial services industry.

The Complexity Habit

There are certain features of The Complexity Habit that can trap the unwary. How caught up are you in that tangled web and what can you do about it? Here are some simple questions to help shine a light on this malady.

Below, rate yourself on a scale from 1 - 5 on how accurate the statements are—1 means 'not accurate at all', and 5 means 'most accurate'. Once you've rated yourself for each statement, total up your scores and then use the Answer Key to determine your next steps.

	Statement	Score
1.	When things aren't working I tend to jump in and learn as much as I can.	______
2.	I agree with the old saying 'knowledge is power'.	______
3.	In my experience, big problems warrant big solutions.	______
4.	My advisers must be, above all else, highly technically credentialed.	______
5.	To combat being misinformed, I really need to get my head around the details.	______
6.	When I sink my teeth into a project I tend to bite off more than I can chew.	______
7.	My pet peeve is inefficiency or something not working properly.	______
8.	It's important to make the best decision possible.	______
9.	Attempts to optimise my finances have resulted in dead ends.	______
10.	I feel anxious that I'm running out of time to solve my finance problems.	______

11. I don't like leaving problems unsolved, especially if they're important. __________
12. I get satisfaction from beating them at their own game. __________
13. I often lose track of time when I'm looking into something online. __________
14. When faced with a problem, my 'go-to' strategy is DIY research. __________
15. Rarely in my experience do elegant, simple solutions have a lasting effect. __________
16. People call me persistent, focussed, or determined. __________
17. I tend towards obsessive when it comes to problem solving. __________

Total Score __________

What Your Score Really Means

Score: 0 – 24

Ready for results

Although some of these tendencies leave you open to the Complexity Habit, it's not causing you undue difficulty right now. This means you're ready to take on some strategies and ideas that will become your new normal, to create the results you crave in your financial world. You're a blank canvas– so chin up!

Score: 25 – 59

Overthinking isn't helpful here

As you read through the pages that follow, try to keep that epithet in mind because your first reaction might be to second-guess the framework. Hey—that's totally okay, but let me reassure you: you don't need to 'white-knuckle the steering wheel'. You're on the right track.

Your first task is going to be pulling back out of the weeds to a 50,000-foot view. Being able to see your bigger picture in this way immediately relaxes your grip because you don't have to hold on to everything for fear of it falling on the floor. From here the view is just dandy: you can see it all unfolding in front of you, everything in view.

As you start to get a handle on your 'GPS', a concept you'll read about in Chapter 6, you will begin feeling more comfortable about trusting the process and letting go a little bit, which will reduce friction in the system. Results will start to flow for you.

Score: 60+

Analytics is your superpower

You and I have something in common, my dear friend. Although our superpower has got us out of trouble more often than not, and won us accolades and a feeling of satisfaction, perfectionism is our Achilles' Heel, especially when it comes to finance and financial planning.

Rarely does the financial services industry offer solutions that are simple and elegant, which gives you the opportunity to really engage with the details. Trouble is, while you're wrapped around the axle of all that complexity, you're being quietly fleeced.

Don't let mastering the science of this distract you from getting results. My advice to you, dear reader, is not to let perfect get in the way of great.

The Pareto Principle that says 80% of your results will come from 20% of your effort and activities is alive and well in financial services. Use it to your advantage because, if you go with your gut and don't follow this Method, you'll find it easier than most to wander off the path, and your results will suffer.

If you keep the 80/20 concept close to your heart as you read this book, you have a better-than-even chance that you'll actually finish it, which is how it is going to deliver you the results you seek. Best of all, this means the results that are waiting for you on the other side of this book are going to be radically different from what you're used to.

Strap in so you can enjoy the ride.

The Magic Pill Culture

In the last chapter you saw how some business owner couples had been side-tracked by this problem. People in business often spend their entire day reaching into their bag of magic tricks and pulling out the proverbial rabbit to solve someone else's problem, which can include:

- Getting clients across the line who've suddenly developed a decision-making disability
- Sweet-talking a supplier who you really wanted to throttle because she promised delivery two weeks ago
- Smoothing things over with a creditor who woke up on the wrong side of bed and felt like pulling the carpet out from under you

Sound familiar? And this is all before 11:30 in the morning! I often joke that the typical business owner walks on water twice a day before lunchtime.

We live in a magic pill culture. Take this pill, it cures your headache. "*Great, I can get back to what I was doing.*"

What do you do, though, when the headache keeps returning? Time to see a doctor. Ugh. It's time consuming, it's expensive, and inconvenient. But just in case it's brain cancer, you go.

The symptom is recurrent headaches. If you're lucky, you'll discover the cause, and the cause is treatable. With a pill? Or is the necessary treatment a change in lifestyle? God, I hope it's a pill.

Turns out you've got a head-banging lifestyle, which means the only way to assure yourself of a headache-free existence is to change your lifestyle. *"Ugh! Maybe I can put up with the headaches!"*

If our magic pill culture has soaked itself into your fabric, it's very likely this has happened because you're a pretty capable person, but you're probably also over-stretched. Ever heard the saying 'if you want to get anything done, give it to the busiest person you know'? That's you.

The Magic Pill Culture

There are certainly plenty of examples showing how this tendency has major payoffs in our culture. In planning and optimising your finances, though, it can work against you.

Here are some simple questions to help you work that out. Below, rate yourself on a scale from 1 - 5 on how accurate the statements are—1 means 'not accurate at all', and 5 means most accurate'. Once you've rated yourself for each statement, total up your scores and then use the Answer Key to determine your next steps.

	Statement	Score
1.	Making decisions is not my problem.	________
2.	Momentum is important.	________
3.	Attempts to optimise my finances have been frustrating stops and starts.	________
4.	I tend to over-extend myself which leads to having too many projects.	________
5.	I've been described as ambitious.	________
6.	My pet peeve is slow drivers.	________
7.	I expect my advisers to see things from a bigger perspective.	________
8.	My Achilles' Heel is implementation—I'm great at strategy, lousy at follow through.	________
9.	I find attending to details more tiring than dealing with something and moving on.	________
10.	I'm great at dealing with the problem at hand.	________
11.	When the next problem comes up, I'll deal with that too.	________
12.	I can often be disappointed by the performance of others.	________

13. It annoys me when people can't make a decision or over-analyse the problem. ____________
14. My financial anxiety is around lack of a cohesive, comprehensive solution. ____________
15. I do tend to overwork myself, sometimes to exhaustion. ____________
16. My finances weren't built to a master-blueprint, they just sort of evolved. ____________

Total Score ____________

What Your Score Really Means

Score:0–19
The blank canvas

The good news is that this is not your problem. As you get deeper into this approach, it's likely to easily resonate with you and executing the Method will feel straightforward and sensible. The risk, though, because this particular Magic Pill hurdle is not yours, is that you'll skip important sections or miss key messages. Don't short-change yourself. Read what's here and profit by it. Read on.

Score: 21–54
Action Jackson

This isn't your particular brand of kryptonite, but your results might be being held back from really helping you to soar like an eagle.

I'm willing to bet, too, that if you've received advice before, it's probably not provided any sort of lasting benefits. There is a very good reason for this—it was symptom-based, not goal-based. This is very common in financial services which generally employs this self-serving symptomatic approach to prioritise its interests ahead of yours.

This Method is a holistic and comprehensive framework that leaves nothing to chance and nothing unattended. Like any good solution, it also evolves as with you to help you solve bigger problems as you move through the journey.

Score: 55+
The quarterback

"*Throw me the ball, I've got this.*" Your skill and confidence are great assets in your career and in life. The danger you face, Mr/Mrs Remarkably Capable Person, lies in your potential to do yourself incredible damage by racing down the wrong road at a million miles an hour.

It takes a while to discover that a dead end is actually a dead end. Worse, because you're a 'can do' person, the risk is you'll get to the dead end and start an excavation program to tunnel through to the other side.

Considering your past experiences, you might find it tough to stick with the program and see this Method through because it's such a comprehensive and enduring solution. That might mean you'll find it a challenge to just follow the bouncing ball. That's okay, built into the program are numerous flag-points that you should keep an eye out for because they'll give you the feedback you need to keep on keeping on.

Forest and Trees Syndrome

Remember Bernie, from the last chapter? He was the retiree who'd lost sight of the forest, all he could see was trees.

What this means is he had got so wrapped up in the problem that the forest was actually just a bunch of trees, and they all looked the same, and all of the branches on each of the trees also looked the same. It was like his vision had blurred, he'd lost the ability to see the bigger picture.

This is something you very likely have experienced yourself. Like, for example, that time you had an argument with your spouse and you got so caught up in your need to win the fight (or at least not to lose) . . . and at some point you suddenly realised you'd forgotten what it was you were arguing about. "*No, I've never had that experience.*" Ha.

Losing sight of the forest tends to happen when something

really matters to us in the moment. We become so focussed on that one thing that we lose sight of the bigger picture and the real reasons we're involved in the first place.

Forest and Trees Syndrome

Are you caught up in Forest and Trees Syndrome? Here are some simple questions to help you break out of that trap if you're stuck.

Below, rate yourself on a scale from 1 - 5 on how accurate the statements are—1 means 'not accurate at all', and 5 means 'most accurate'. Once you've rated yourself for each statement, total up your scores and then use the Answer Key to determine your next steps.

	Statement	Score
1.	I feel at home in the driver's seat.	______
2.	Pet peeve: stupid people.	______
3.	Good advice: ask and ye shall receive.	______
4.	I didn't get to where I am by leaving it to chance.	______
5.	When it comes to decisions that affect my wealth, there's no second chance here.	______
6.	My anxiety is around being taken advantage of or misled.	______
7.	These days, often the only way to distinguish value is by lowest cost.	______
8.	Attempts to optimise any aspect of my finances have proven to be far slower and more obstructed than they should have been.	______
9.	I'm used to achieving what I set out to achieve, one way or another.	______
10.	When relying on others, I expect results as good as those I accomplish.	______

11. When I tell someone something, I expect them to do it. ________
12. Capable people are not as common as incapable people. ________
13. Reducing standards to suit the lowest common denominator is a losing strategy. ________
14. I might overthink things, but it has always stood by me when it counted. ________

Total Score ________

What Your Score Really Means

Score: 0–10
Green light

It looks like you're not overly weighed down by this hurdle. 'The Catch' to this Method, explained in Chapter 5, is not likely to come as any surprise to you, and you've got the green light to put your foot to the floor because the chances are that, if this is you, you should find the new ideas and concepts you're going to read in the pages ahead make sense and fall into place.

Score: 11–44
Bob the Builder

Having built a strong asset base hasn't left you jaded, but if you start to feel tense through this process you run the risk of skimming certain sections and missing key messages. Chances are this will come back to haunt you later as you progress in the framework and the fixator in you comes out, grinding your progress to a halt.

Being able to keep your big picture top of mind, when all about you are losing theirs, is not just valuable for people built like Bernie—it's valuable for us all.

You're probably used to getting handed problems that need to be solved before you can resume what you were doing before the interruption. This is also evidence you're immensely capable . . . which unfortunately does have a downside, believe it or not. Because the financial services industry specialises in loading you up with stuff that'll keep you busy.

Let's face it, you didn't get to where you are by losing your head when all around you were also losing theirs.

If you find yourself digging in or getting snagged on a particular sub-quest that you just can't leave alone, remember this: this Method is, at its core, simple. Sure, the book is 12+ chapters long, but what pumps blood through its veins is a very simple machine, and it won't work if you clog it up with too much thinking.

Keep the reins loose in your hands, let the temptation to second-guess where this is going pass you by, and have a little trust in the Method. You're not wasting your time here, I can promise you.

Score: 45+
The cynic

Your hard-won experience has earned you wisdom. It doesn't come without a cost, though, which is a dash of scepticism, even a little sprinkle of cynicism. Good news: the truth is that this can help when it comes to finance because—although it might sounda little harsh—being sceptical about the financial services industry is not unreasonable, frankly.

There is some sobering news, though, and that is you do run the risk of negotiating a pretty cost-effective solution . . . only to find out that it only does half the job because the counter-party to your negotiation didn't realise that the offer wasn't viable in the long run.

The Independent Planning-for-results Method is liberally seasoned with reminders to recall your bigger picture and endgame, for you and your family. This is no bitter pill you're being forced to swallow—there are battles and there are wars, and it's important to be able to tell one from the other when it counts.

Bearing the scars of a battle-weary veteran

How'd you do with the self-assessments above? Some folks are lucky enough to be well acquainted with all three of these particular symptoms, whereas others are burdened by less common ailments.

Regardless of what your scores say about you, we all have one thing in common: we've all had certain experiences, and we've all got the scars to prove it. As a matter of fact, my dear reader, it's reasonably likely that you have more than your fair share. I know I feel that way, some days more than others.

Moving on . . .

The problem lurking beneath the symptoms

We started off this chapter talking about symptoms, that nagging itch we can't scratch. Financially speaking, they might show up like this . . .

> *My **returns** aren't high enough, how do I get higher returns?*
>
> *I'm paying too much in **fees**, how do I reduce them?*
>
> *My **investments** don't fill me with confidence, how do I get better investments?*
>
> *I'm not sure whether my **insurance** is any good, how do I get more comprehensive coverage?*
>
> *I'm paying too much in **tax**, how do I reduce it?*
>
> *I'm not sure my **retirement** nest egg is going to last for life, what do I need to do to get that certainty?*

Left untreated, these symptoms create worry and anxiety that metastasise into other areas of your life. It can disrupt your sleep, cause arguments with your spouse, rob you of time for your kids and hobbies and other areas of your life that give you joy.

The fear is that, without a solution, you're stuck in that river Billy Joel sings about, and you won't know any peace. These fears—most assuredly—are genuine. They're real and need to be solved, no mistaking that. But we've done some work here and traced these symptoms back to underlying problems, manifesting as the Complexity Habit, the Magic Pill Culture, and Forest and Trees Syndrome.

What caused these problems though? If we could get at that

cause, somehow, these problems would clear up. The bigger question, then, is what's behind these problems? What do they have in common?

That exercise isn't just time consuming and mentally exhausting, it's tough to dismantle a problem when there are piranhas nipping at your heels. Plus—let's face it—who's got the patience and presence of mind when you've just put in another 10-hour day at your profession and you're being beckoned by a glass of wine and Netflix?

Answer it we must, though, otherwise we'll stay stuck in Groundhog Day.

What's your plan?

Without a plan, you're like a float bobbing around on the ocean, adrift and at sea, subject to wherever the wind and tide take you. Nothing's in your control. Shiny things distract you and anything seems better than what you've got. It's hard to make progress in a world like that.

But if the answer is a plan, something so simple, why has it taken so long to address?

We glimpsed the reason a moment ago—professionally successful family people have a great many demands on their time. They have lots of responsibilities and, of course, there are those piranhas. At the end of a long day it's very hard to solve big problems when you've got little left in the tank.

> *"If only I had the time to get organised, do all the research, and work it all out."*

Ah. There you have it.

There's actually a very good and simple reason why you don't have a plan, or if you do, why it's not working very well. The penny has dropped: you can now turn your attention to a solution that actually gets at the cause, which will solve the problem and evaporate the symptoms.

Next chapter I'll show you what that looks like.

Ah ha's . . .

- *As reasonable, intelligent, successful adults, we each have a natural tendency that we tend to gravitate towards when solving a big problem. In the world of finance, these most often show up as the Complexity Habit, the Magic Pill Culture, and the Forest and Trees Syndrome.*
- *The financial services industry knows this and uses it as a business model to keep us on the hamster wheel. The key to breaking free of this cycle is simple but counter-intuitive, which is why so many remain overwhelmed and stuck.*
- *Not having a good plan is the single biggest factor preventing consistent, desirable results. Remove this roadblock and your likelihood of better results is significantly improved, immediately.*

Chapter 4

The Reasons Why This Method Works

"For every minute spent organising an hour is earned."
—Benjamin Franklin

The secret key to this Method

I've mentioned the Pareto Principle already—it's a wonderful idea discovered by an Italian mathematician who proposed that 80% of your results can be traced back to just 20% of what you're doing.

What many people presume this means, incorrectly, is that they can just do the 20% and skip the rest, hoping to get the same results. Not so.

But getting that 20% right is going to lift an awful lot of the load for you. So in this chapter, we're going to be exploring what that 20% is and why it is so important to get the full benefit of what this Method offers.

Let's quickly recap, though: what have we discovered so far?

We've established that you're a capable, intelligent person, worried about an aspect of your finances. So much so, it's starting to make you feel anxious and uncertain about your family's financial future.

Being a responsible adult, you've made various attempts to solve what you think is the problem, but so far this hasn't dispelled the anxiety, or if it has, not for long. This is because what's bothering you about your finances is just a symptom, not really the cause. This explains why getting your questions answered doesn't seem to bring any lasting relief to the itch you're trying to scratch.

The reality is that the underlying cause of the problem is that something's missing: the cure for uncertainty is a good plan.

If that's the conclusion, then you'd be well within your rights to wonder why you don't have one. Certainly you're smart enough. You're also old enough. Is it the pace of life? Is it not knowing where to start? What's prevented you from developing a plan?

"Just disorganised, I guess."

And so we arrive at the heart of the matter, what *unlocks the entire system and makes it work.*

If you were to take nothing else from this book but the message to *get organised financially,* that alone would provide you a massive boost in what you're trying to accomplish.

Being disorganised is not only not your fault, it's absolutely to be expected when it comes to finance. There is a stunning body of information out there, one swamped by an even bigger body of misinformation. The noise that distracts and misdirects, the hidden agendas of predators who want to sell you stuff ... I'm amazed anyone gets anywhere at all, considering these obstacles.

A new perspective

Overcoming these hurdles starts by looking at your current financial situation and your financial future through *a new lens.*

You see, your finances don't exist for their own benefit. Their purpose is to enable you to experience your desired style of life—your ideal lifestyle. I didn't say a fantasy lifestyle of the rich and famous. I meant a lifestyle that fits your ideal. Or, to put it another way, *your finances enable your best life.*

Unless you're lucky, a 'best life' doesn't happen by chance. It happens by design, specifically by designing your financial life. That means planning. Planning your future as part of a process that gets your financial life 100% *organised* makes your finances effectively bulletproof, which means your best life is assured.

If there is one 'secret key' that underpins the entire framework of the Independent Planning-for-results Method, it's the principle of getting financially organised. **Get your 'financial house' in order** and you will start to realise that optimising your finances to get better returns, less risk, lower costs, reduced tax, better investments, no fees . . . they'll all take care of themselves. It's part and parcel of that process of getting your financial house in perfect order. By definition.

When you can get your head around this line of thinking, that simple concept of getting financially organised opens up entire new vistas about how you can chart your way to the horizon without having to crack the nut of the uncontrollable financial services industry.

Everyone's out chasing high returns, less risk, reduced fees, better investments, more comprehensive insurance. It's a very magic pill, product-driven approach, and the financial services industry thrives on ensuring you get lost in the weeds. Get your Financial House in order and the knock-on benefit is these ideal outcomes happen as a natural result of the process.

When you are 100% organised and confident about your family's future finances, you're effectively financially bulletproof, able to withstand any economic meltdown or global crisis, plus you have a clear line-of-sight that you're on track to achieve all your most important goals.

But it even goes further than that . . .

Poor planning, incomplete planning, or no planning at all . . . generally, that's only revealed in times of crisis. And crisis management is no way to live a life. Getting organised means that all the risks have been addressed—you have a plan A, plan B, and others besides.

That is what gives you a sense of confidence. *That* is what dispels the anxiety and worry. *That* is what creates certainty out of chaos.

The key that opens the door

In the last chapte,r we looked at some couples who were having that experience. They used the Independent Planning-for-results Method to transform chaos into certainty, anxiety into confidence.

Transform these symptoms . . .	**into these solutions**
• They felt anxious or exposed or disorganised or vulnerable or beholden. • They recognised there is a great deal of time and complexity involved in navigating the money management industry. • They felt they had insufficient time, expertise/qualifications or connections to be confident they'd do a good job. • They don't want to feel foolish for stuffing this up, making a costly and very public mistake.	• They started to develop a sense of clarity, direction, certainty, and progress towards measurable and visible results. • They were planning their future so that it comes to pass intentionally and 'on purpose' rather than let Lady Luck take the wheel. (They save their spontaneity for holidays and adventures.) • They started to feel complete confident that they have a plan, it is a good plan, and they are making strong progress on that plan.

• They were particularly mindful of being told BS by a slick salesman, being taken advantage of, misled, or losing their money through poor decisions.	• They developed relationships with people they could trust to be involved in their planning and help play a role in getting better results.
• They certainly didn't want to feel lost or directionless anymore but also didn't want to waste their time going down dead ends or making costly wrong turns.	• They experienced more time freedom so they could focus on enjoying the experiences life has to offer with those people who are important to them.
• They weren't looking forward to discovering they'd been needlessly wasting money in hidden high fees in products that take unpublished risks with their money.	• They could see tangible evidence of being more organised and on track, and that if the unexpected happens or events beyond their control happen, their future is still assured.

Get this into your bones. The extent that you embed this new awareness into your psyche is the same extent to which you will get what you want more quickly and more simply than you previously believed possible.

So now you know, and now you know why: you live your best life by design rather than by chance, and getting your finances organised is how you do it. The truth is that getting organised financially won't just answer today's question, it'll answer tomorrow's as-yet-unasked questions, too.

The rooms of your Financial House

Organising your finances first requires breaking them down into bite-sized chunks.

Your home consists of a number of rooms, each with a place and a purpose. All homes have nuances, but you can probably break a house down into five main functions:

- Sleeping
- Cooking/eating
- Living/entertainment
- Washing/toileting
- Laundering/cleaning

Leave any of them out—toileting, for example—and you'll notice there's something missing pretty quickly. Also, some of the rooms in your house have common features—for instance the kitchen and laundry are both 'wet areas'—this needs to be considered when designing the house if you want to do it economically and efficiently.

Your financial house consists of five different types of rooms, too. You have rooms for your . . .

1. Cash
2. Wealth
3. Tax
4. Legals
5. Risks

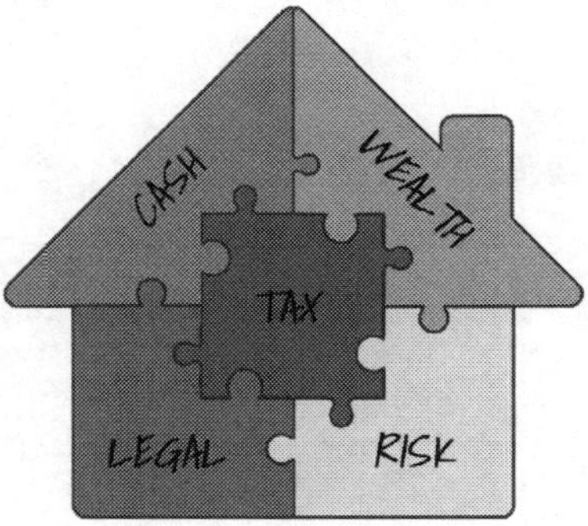

Just like the house you live in, omit any one of these rooms from your Financial House and you'll notice it sooner or later. For instance, when contemplating their finances, people often make the mistake thinking it's all about investing. That's an essential activity in creating wealth, for sure, but frankly its importance is not as significant as you might think. If, for instance, you neglect the risks your financial house is quietly exposed to, you may well come to regret it.

Each of these rooms consists of a number of activities. Add the word 'planning' to each of those room names and you can start to see how those activities line up.

"Good planning is important."

—Edmund Hillary

Cash planning

Cash planning covers things like your cashflows (the ins and outs of your money each month), your banking arrangements (where that cash gets allocated and how you access it when you need it), credit and finance (which you use to acquire assets that grow in value or depreciate in value), the operation of your investments and retirement accounts and your entitlements to social security.

There is an old saying in business—regardless of your profits, cash is king. Cash is first in the list because it is usually something that happens automatically and habitually. Get it wrong and you will notice quickly. Get it right and it feels like you have the wind at your back.

> *"Annual income twenty pounds, annual expenditure nineteen nineteen and six , result happiness. Annual income twenty pounds, annual expenditure twenty pounds ought and six, result misery."*
>
> **—Charles Dickens, *David Copperfield***

Wealth planning

Planning wealth includes goal setting and establishing how to fund those goals through investment planning, planning for retirement and the costs of aged care, 'what if' analysis which uses financial modelling and forecasting techniques to explore best, worst and most likely scenarios.

> *"Provide in advance for the needs of thy growing age and the protection of thy family."*
>
> **—George Samuel Clason,**
> ***The RichestMan in Babylon***

Tax planning

Although there is a saying that 'tax is the price a civilized community pays to remain civilised', there is another saying along the lines of 'only a fool pays more tax than is necessary'. Tax planning includes legally minimising liabilities as well as ensuring the liabilities are calculated in advance, fully funded by earmarking future reserves cash. It includes accounting, tax returns, and sensible structuring of business and investment entities.

> *"In this world, nothing is certain but death and taxes."*
>
> **—Benjamin Franklin**

Legal planning

The law, they say, is the second oldest profession, and it is foolhardy indeed for a couple to leave themselves legally unprotected. This is particularly true when you're disadvantaged or compromised through incapacity, or deceased. Tasks covered in this subject include mapping out your estate, establishing an estate inventory, drawing up your wills and other legal documents such as medical care directives and powers of attorney. Legal planning includes many other specialisations whose relevance to you will depend on your income-producing activities.

> *"The end of law is not to abolish or restrain, but to preserve and enlarge freedom."*
>
> **—John Locke**

Risk planning

Certainly this covers things like life and general insurances, but there's more to risk planning than having the right insurance policies.

When you set a goal—particularly a long term, meaningful and significant financial goal—you want to have the highest confidence you're on track and that, if anything doesn't go according to plan, there's a 'Plan B' to get you back on track. Risk planning is about thinking of all the possible obstacles, roadblocks, risks and weaknesses that might delay, defer or even deny your goal.

Done properly, risk planning means continuously asking three key questions: 'what can go wrong?', 'how likely is it?' and 'what are the consequences if it does?'. Issues like the security of your documents (including your identity) fall into this category, as does electronic theft and fraud—these can rob you quicker and more profoundly than a sour investment.

"Measure twice, cut once."

—carpenters' saying

Getting your Financial House in order

As you cast your eyes back over this list of rooms to your Financial House, can you start to imagine how, if you were to tidy up each room and get it properly organised, you would also have answers to all the money questions that prompted you to pick up this book in the first place? Recall that these are the same questions we established were symptomatic of not having a plan.

Better than just being organised, once each of the rooms of your financial house is properly organised—we're talking 10 out of 10—your finances are actually **bulletproof**, by definition.

More than that, even, *by bulletproofing your finances, you give certainty to your financial future into the bargain. Today's finances are bulletproof and so are tomorrow's.*

We'll get deeper into these subjects in future chapters, but for now the key point to fix in your mind is that, if you embrace the principle of getting organised financially, then you'll give yourself the highest probability you can have to experience the future you desire.

Ah ha's . . .

- *In a nutshell, optimising your finances means getting your Financial House in order, which in turn gives you a bulletproof financial future.*
- *Problems like the Complexity Habit, the Magic Pill Culture and Forest and Trees Syndrome are problems that can prevent you from making real progress.*
- *Seeking answers to disparate finance questions is treating the symptom, not the cause. There is no clearer sign of 'no good plan' than this list of questions.*
- *Developing the best plan, then, starts by looking at the rooms of your Financial House. That is, simplify your finances into five bite-sized subjects.*
- *Setting each of those rooms into proper order is the key to financial certainty and confidence.*

Chapter 5

What's the Catch?

"Every decision we make in life,
there's always a cost."

—Brad Meltzer

Your investment in getting organised

There is a price tag to getting organised. This can be a hurdle for some: "*It sounds like a lot of work, and it's probably expensive.*"

There is no shortage of options, either, when it comes to getting financial planning advice, as a casual stroll through any airport bookstore will reveal rows of shelves entirely devoted to the topic.

In this chapter, I'm going to confront the elephant in the room: what is the cost of becoming organised and what other options are available to you?

In fact, let's start with the latter.

What's wrong with other approaches

At this point, you might be feeling a bit disheartened. Perhaps you've read a book, done a course on-line. Perhaps you've even had a financial adviser for years but aren't getting anything like the benefits I've described so far.

Why aren't the other approaches working for you?

Books that fall short

I'm a huge consumer of 'information products', particularly when it comes to finance. In fact, much of what you can find in the business, finance, or self-help section of the bookstore is on my shelves or my Kindle.

If you too are a veteran of this genre, you will also have noticed the same ideas cropping up again and again, recycled by the same author in their other books, or even in the books of other authors who are rebranding concepts they read about somewhere else.

In my experience, these books tend to be one-dimensional. They explore a particular aspect of finance and most commonly it's the same theme: how to make money. There are two established angles on this age-old formula: the turtle and the fox.

The turtle

Slow, safe, secure. The way to accumulate wealth is to learn these budgeting strategies, spend less than you earn, syphon part of that into investments, and let the magical power of compound interest do its work for you. There's always a bit in there about Einstein's alleged quote on how compound interest is the 8th wonder of the world, too.

The fox

Stealthy, clever, quick. The path to rapid riches lies in acquiring this author's Midas Touch secrets. Each author has a proprietary name but it boils down to their allegedly successful share trading tips, a property investing program, ideas on crypto or gold.

Don't take my word for it—get onto Amazon and have a browse yourself. Before your tenth book, I promise you, you'll be able to see this formula at play.

I'm not saying that no other published book has any value except the one you're reading now. As I've already pointed out, finance is a broad subject filled with complexity that will keep the technophile engaged for many decades. The elements of finance—budgeting, tax, investing, the effect of compound interest—are most certainly essential pieces of furniture in your Financial House. But they're pieces of the puzzle, not the picture the puzzle is supposed to make.

You can read lots of these books and absorb a lot of knowledge about the machinations and technical aspects of how particular aspects of finance work. But it doesn't get you organised. Which means it doesn't get you certainty about your future.

Courses that miss the mark

I used to enjoy attending courses when I was younger. I'd read all the prep material and organise my thoughts, I'd gobble up the material on the day and then debrief to put the ideas into action. When the online thing started I was in heaven.

Hey, don't judge me. Some people did cocaine, I did courses. So shut up.

One thing you notice after you've been through a few is the theatre that's involved. Makes sense—there's a presenter and an audience, so theatre is the appropriate label. The best presenters who put on the best stage shows are following well-crafted scripts, and the theatre of the online course is no exception.

The show opens with something called 'The Hero's Journey', which is the presenter's opportunity to tell their story so that it resonates with yours. In the sales cycle, that's the first step, removing the obstacle called 'no trust'. I could go into the necessary elements for a good story—a charismatic protagonist, an urgent quest, the hero's dilemma . . . but I think you get the idea.

Anyway, the point is that these programs are primarily infotainment. This is the reason why you come away from a course all pumped up but two weeks later you've forgotten about it. As good as the material might be, as powerful as the presenter is, generally you don't experience any lasting change. That can't get you organised. Which means it doesn't get you certainty about your future.

Seeking advice from Claytons Financial planners

There is a type of kola tonic called 'Claytons' which, for many years, was marketed as the non-alcoholic alternative when you feel like having a drink but shouldn't. The catchphrase was: "*Claytons. The drink you have when you're not having a drink.*"

In Australia, a nation with a well-deserved reputation for

big drinkers, the name Claytons became slang for anything considered a shoddy substitute.

Here's an insider's tip: many financial planners are nothing of the sort—not in the way I'm talking about in this book, at any rate.

They might call their services 'holistic' and promise comprehensive advice, but at the end of the day, they're more interested in onboarding you into their investment program and, almost as an afterthought, giving you some generic advice to buy some insurance and get your wills up to date.

I should know, that's what I was taught a million years ago when I first became a financial adviser. I don't begrudge it at all, to be honest—after all, it was my frustration with that empty promise in the early days that motivated me to develop the Method I'm teaching you in this book today.

This cohort of financial advisers are really investment consultants. Nothing wrong with that, but why call a spade a shovel unless you've got an agenda? And frankly, in my experience, that hidden agenda is that most financial planning firms are actually 'funds under management' businesses who charge a percentage of whatever you invest in exchange for a promise that only appeals to the naïve.

According to statistics, one in five adults seek advice from a financial planner. It's my bet that one in five readers of these words know precisely what I'm talking about in the scenario I've described above. The empty promise I've described gets you a product but it doesn't get you organised. Which means it doesn't get you certainty about your future.

A sea of information

Hey, take heart: it's not your fault these approaches didn't accomplish lasting results. Let me be clear about what I'm saying here . . .

Books, courses, websites, financial advisers, blogs, newsletters, subscription services—these are all legitimate sources of information and there's nothing wrong with that. Information has its place. Let's not confuse knowledge and wisdom, though, which gets you worthwhile results.

You can spend a lifetime accumulating information, but that doesn't necessarily translate into smart choices, which is what's so valuable about wisdom. One way of looking at wisdom is that it's the accumulation of lessons learned by making poor choices.

The experience of making poor choices can be painful, but if you learn from these mistakes, they can be priceless beyond measure. There is another very valuable way to accumulate wisdom and that's by learning from the mistakes of others. Not as painful but really helpful in avoiding that same mistake.

The evolution of this Method was shaped in part by addressing the disadvantages inherent in your other options. There's a sea of information out there, but frankly, you don't have the time to master it all. What you need is the benefit of that information, rather than the information itself. That's wise. *That* can get you organised, and *That* can get you certainty about your future.

The price of wisdom

One issue that some people might struggle with is the imagined price tag attached to getting organised. Let's confront this head-on.

There's no sugarcoating this: yes, there's work involved. If you don't want to do the work, you can pay someone to do most of it for you. Either way, someone has to do something. You know this already from your own experience: any worthwhile accomplishment requires some outlay of time, money, effort, sacrifice, thinking, or a combination of all of these.

That said, hear this warning: *looking at this process as a cost is a very expensive mistake to make*. It's not a 'sunk cost', you see. Getting organised is an investment and you can expect a return. A big one.

This isn't just semantics. There is an ROI that comes in two forms—actual tangible cash and intangible personal value.

The cash ROI

Let's look at the cash first.

Reduced fees (better net result), reduced risk (no disasters), more stable returns (better compounding effect), reduced tax, avoided penalties, etc.

If you have a home loan, you'd expect that being organised means you've got the most sensible structure and rate for you, that you're making the best use of offset accounts, and that the loan gets paid off as soon as it's possible to do. This saves you interest and fees. What's that worth this year and over the next ten years?

If you have an investment, you'd expect that being organised means you're not gambling with your money so your risks of loss are reduced, your costs of management are reduced to the lowest fees/value for money, there are no middlemen taking a cut, unnecessary platform fees, and so on. What might this combination of lower costs and higher returns translate to in terms of improved outcomes over the next twenty years?

Turning to your insurances, if you were fully organised in that room of your Financial House, your coverage would be water-tight, your premiums lower, etc, etc. The next time disaster strikes, the insurance company isn't hunting for loopholes in your policy, they're paying out. How often do you claim on your policies—once a year? Once a decade?

You get the idea. If you're attentive, it takes no imagination at all to see a return on your investment.

The personal payoff

Pardon the pun but—for my money—the intangible benefits are where the **real** value lies.

What's the worry and anxiety and uncertainty costing you at the moment in lost sleep, drained energy, misunderstandings and arguments, regret and shame, disconnection and hopelessness?

Now let's flip that around . . . what are the benefits to the end of that?

Where there was worry, there is now a feeling of certainty.
Where there was anxiety, there is now confidence and optimism and hope.
How much better do you sleep?
How grounded are you so you neatly sidestep the arguments?
How much more patience do you suddenly have for your spouse and your kids because there's no imagined disaster looming?

I'm not being dramatic—this is real. The chances are pretty good you know very well what I'm talking about.

This is the key to feeling like part of a team again with your spouse and part of a family again with your kids (instead of an unappreciated slave!).

Do you have the clarity and money to finance the next holiday? You want to go because you love them, it's not an escape from your jail cell, it's a reward for your being organised. Where did that money come from? You haven't had to take a second job. Your investment in being more organised is starting to yield results.

> *"There are risks and costs to a program of action. But they are far less than the long-range risks and costs of comfortable inaction."*
>
> **—John F. Kennedy**

The cost of not getting organised

Let's look at this the other way around.

Is there really any alternative? I mean, seriously, after all the territory we've covered, do you have any other choice at this point but to go ahead and do this for yourself?

Look, if you accept that . . .

1. You're better off with a plan than without a plan, and
2. What's keeping you from having a plan is getting organised, then
3. Your choice is either to do nothing and stay disorganised (and stay in the state you're in), or just do it—simply get organised, once and for all.

The alternative to doing this is not doing this. To leave it alone is to let Lady Luck take the wheel. That might have been fun when we were teenagers, but as 40-to-60-somethings with successful careers and families, is that really where we're coming from?

Not to labour the point, but let's get specific . . .

The emotional cost

The cost of not getting organised means staying in the state you're in. The low-level, ever-present worry that grows into anxieties . . . leads to catastrophising at 3am . . . leads to poor sleep . . . which deletes resources you're going to need to do your job, be tolerant with demands from kids and responsive to the needs of others, especially your spouse.

How long can you bear this burden before the cracks start to appear like our friend the business owner who is now taking antidepressants?

The economic cost

How much potential wealth will you 'leave on the table'? Costs that could have been reduced, returns that could have improved, fees and expenses that should have been lower. And that's only if nothing goes wrong!

If one of the risks that would have been attended to had you been organised actually knocks on your door, does that mean you're now reliant on family, friends or—worse—the government? Is that going to get easier or harder in your declining years?

Just hyperbole?

Look, my dear reader, I don't want to lose you here, but I'm not doing my job if I sugarcoat this stuff. The statistics on this picture are unarguable. Don't take my word for it—do the Googling yourself.

There is a direct, causal link between money problems and marriage breakups and family breakdowns. Ask any single parent whether this is what they had in mind when they first fell in love with the person they now call their 'ex'. Honestly, the stories of disagreements and their slippery slope to chronic marital disharmony, as well as stuff you only read about—domestic violence, infidelity, substance abuse . . . it's real. Do the reading at your peril—it's enough to send shivers down your spine.

You might think these stories have nothing to do with you. They're galaxies away. But remember this: it only takes one major event to quantum-shift you into a completely different and perilous orbit. An event that should have been attended to in the process of getting financially organised.

It's such an ugly picture. And a completely avoidable one, too.

A rosier picture

Getting organised puts you back in the driver's seat, where you belong. Getting organised gives you a great shot at clarity, direction, confidence and certainty. Not only does this enhance your financial outlook, it improves the outlook for your children (and their children) into the bargain. It is statistically likely to have some sort of continuing, positive effect on your mental health, your marriage, and your physical well-being, leaving you free to focus on what's truly important to you.

It really is like winning the jackpot.

Is there really any choice? I can't imagine that you'd have read this far if you weren't convinced so I'm now going to assume you've made the decision that getting organised is not a 'want' but a 'must have'.

Earlier I warned about the risk of confusing knowledge and wisdom. There is another mistake I'd like to warn you about, and that is you can have all the wisdom in the world, but without action it's not particularly valuable.

The next obvious question is "*Where do I start*?."

That means it's time to get into the Method itself so you can get the results you want. Let's go.

Ah ha's . . .

- *The catch to getting organised is making the investment.*
- *There are big, big returns in the offing, both tangible and intangible, if you're prepared to make the investment in yourself.*
- *The alternative to making the investment is doing nothing. The likely outcomes of comfortable inaction, however, are unthinkable.*

Part 2

How to Bullet-proof Your Finances to Have a More Certain Future.

Unpacking the Independent Planning-for-results Method . . .

In the resources section at the end of this book is a link to download the bonuses that came with this book. There you'll find all the worksheets and templates if the mood takes you to follow along with the exercises in these chapters.

Chapter 6

The Backbone of This Method

"Deciding what not to do is as important as deciding what to do."

—Steve Jobs

In Chapter 4 we explored the key secret and principle that underpins this process of getting great results, namely the concept of *getting your Financial House in order.* Next chapter, we're going to start unpacking the Independent Planning-for-results Method by showing you the three phases of the Method and how they fit together to deliver you predictable results that bulletproof your finances and remove uncertainty about your financial future.

But before we do this, we're going to unveil the core mechanism of the process because this particular tool does a lot of heavy lifting for you all the way through the Method. It is the backbone of the entire process because it holds the three phases of the program, the meat on the bones, together.

It's called your *Global Positioning System,* or 'GPS' for short.

Your Global Positioning System

Your GPS is the IP4R Method's go-to tool as you start to roll out this process. It's your 'where am I now?' device, your to-do list, your journal, your sticky-note reminders, your key to getting and staying organised. Very soon, this is going to become your best friend.

Just like the GPS you might use in your car, the GPS you use in your planning has multiple functions. Think about it this way . . .

Your car's GPS tells you where you are relative to your destination, but it also estimates your time of arrival and a lot of other information like terrain or weather warnings, advance notice if the traffic ahead is gridlocked, alternative routes if there are roadworks ahead, etc.

The best GPS systems take all the guesswork out of your journey. Once you've decided on your destination and turn it on, you don't have to worry anymore—if you take a wrong turn or there's a change in circumstances, the GPS will tell you and find you an alternative route to arrive at your destination safely. Recalibrate.

So too, your IP4RM GPS takes all the guesswork and worry out of your head and puts it into one easy-to-use place. You don't have to think about it. You just have to open it and do the next thing on the list.

A live plan of action

It's your living, working plan that serves as a one-stop-shop for all the due dates, action items, key milestones, goal due dates, scheduled meetings, and more.

Have you ever got advice from a financial adviser before? The financial plan they give you is generally a huge document full of generic text, tables and fine print that spans many, many pages—sometimes hundreds—and is out of date very quickly. In fact, there's usually a warning written into them that states the advice will expire within a month or so and can't be relied on if you read it beyond that date.

It's for these reasons financial plans often end up in the bottom drawer, never seen again. They have a very short shelf life and no real utility as an ongoing tool to help keep you on track like a living breathing document.

Your GPS, on the other hand, is used by members of your team (more on them later) as a way of keeping track of what needs to be done, by whom, and by when. It is also a central repository for any recommendations or advice that is obtained from 'Subject Matter Experts' (we'll also come back to this in a later part of the book). The GPS becomes a useful way for your team members to communicate with each other while they pursue your vision for your 'life by design'.

You know how just thinking about exercise doesn't make you physically fit, it's the doing that gets the results? Your GPS is the link between your planning and your results. Adopt and embrace the habit of using it as your go-to for all things future and all things financial.

Whatever goes into your GPS . . . happens!

We'll dig deeper into the GPS mechanism later in this book, where I'll also show you how to create your own. For now, though, let's take a look at the concepts-in-practice so you can get a feel for how the GPS works and how you use it to solve the problem of getting (and staying) organised.

In a nutshell anything you write down in your GPS needs to happen. Here are some examples . . .

Make your bucket list real

Get your bucket list into the GPS. If you haven't got a bucket list, then you're missing out. This is high on the priority list and clear evidence you're making progress towards getting organised.

For instance, anytime you have an idea about something you'd like to do one day, some experience you'd like to have, some place you'd like to see: jump into your GPS, scroll down to the next 'progress meeting' (more on this next chapter), and add it to the agenda.

Now it's on paper (or e-paper), and can be 'deep planned', rather than bothering you and causing you to feel like you're missing out on something. When the time comes to give this some serious thought, that's when you decide whether you want to act on it, and if you do, you can relax in the sure knowledge that it's going to happen because it's part of your IP4R Method.

Dream . . . Do

Got a future event that's on your mind, like a child's wedding one day? Get it in your GPS. Want to do something really nice to celebrate an important date? Get it in your GPS. Some ideas that fit nicely here:

- A new car, caravan, or holiday home.
- A 50th birthday gift to yourself of that Rolex watch you've been walking past for years, or a 30th anniversary mega-diamond necklace.
- An overseas holiday to celebrate your daughter's graduation (including turning left as you board the aircraft to enjoy travelling at 'the pointy end').
- That water feature sculpture that really sets up the front entry of your home.

Keep dreaming, you get the idea. Make this fun—on your next date night, add this to the agenda: "*What 'stuff' would we like to have in our lives that would be indulgent and would enrich our experience with a bit of fun?*"

Take it a step further and ask what experiences you'd like the kids (or grandkids) to have that would have the potential to change the course of their lives?

The end of procrastination

Part of the human condition is not doing what you're supposed to be doing when you're supposed to be doing it. It only becomes a problem if it starts to show up often enough to affect your daily life. Often in these moments, we succumb to an impulse to surf the web and find ourselves wandering through recipes on Pinterest, scrolling through Amazon or eBay looking for Christmas present ideas, or looking at the latest post from some special interest group we're following on Facebook.

Anytime you indulge your curiosity in this way, ask yourself whether there's anything important enough to warrant a second look—is this something you'd like to do strive for in your future? If so, add the question to the next 'on the fly' agenda, a running list of everything important that is exercising your mind.

The end of unexpected or unpleasant expenses

We've all had the experience of opening the mail and getting an adrenaline-hit at the shocking size of the bill you weren't expecting. We might find expenses unpleasant but it's not really the expense that's the problem because the cost has a flip side—whatever benefit we got from that outlay was either necessary or enjoyable.

- Rates notice? Someone picks up the garbage bin every Wednesday morning.
- Insurance premium? We're covered if something goes wrong.

So the real problem isn't the cost, it's the "*Ugh! Where is the money coming from to pay this?*"

Imagine that every bill you open has already been factored into your cashflows, there's money sitting there waiting for that particular bill to arrive and pay it, on time and in full. You'd almost be looking forward to it arriving because you've prepared for it, you've been waiting for it . . . and finally here it is. Now that it can be dealt with happily, it's not a problem, not another weight on your shoulders, not another worry about scarcity. This is called being organised.

Next time you come across a bill that you didn't expect or are tired of seeing, add it to the GPS for discussion. Should it be in your life at all? If it should be, how can it be automated so you don't have to bother with it, and how can the funding for it be arranged in advance so it doesn't cause you another moment's distress (no matter how minor)?

The end of anxiety

Psychologists tell us that this feeling we call anxiety is a thought about an imagined future which hasn't been properly interrogated that it metastasises into something hideous.

As captain of your ship, you can catch that thought/notion/fear/worry early. Haul its ass up into the light of your GPS so that it can be properly examined at the appropriate time. If there is any truth to it whatsoever, then there's a process in your IP-4RM to unpack it and solve it.

You're no longer going to tolerate another moment of lost

sleep because these worries don't live in your head anymore. They're in the GPS to be dealt with in an orderly way, using a process that deals with them absolutely, no exceptions. There is no problem, worry, concern, or rumination that can't be lifted off your shoulders and dropped into a place where it can be dealt with using the processes in this book.

Decluttering your mind

There's a personal development exercise I did once where the leader asked the group to take out a notepad and empty our minds into it.

Everything we've been meaning to do, everything we should be doing while we were attending that course, everything we had to put on hold, all the stuff in our to do list, everything that it relates to . . . he wanted it all down on paper.

"Clutter is postponed decisions."

—Barbara Hemphill

We wrote and wrote and wrote. Those who finished sooner than the others were asked to go to the back of the room for a coffee break, leaving the rest of us to keep going. We weren't allowed to get up till we were finished. He wanted every single thing we could think of on that notepad.

I can't remember how long I took—it felt like forever, but once I was done . . . I knew peace. I can't tell you how incredible it felt to have that feeling of carefree lightness once it was all out of my head and on a piece of paper. I was walking an inch taller than before the exercise, I swear.

I want you to use the GPS to have the same experience.

The Brain Dump exercise

You're going to create your GPS later in this book, but for now, you're simply going to declutter your head so that what's on your mind can no longer disturb your sleep, garble your thinking, or interrupt your joy in the moment of whatever you're doing with whoever you're with.

What you're going to do with this list comes later, but for now, the job is to ensure you no longer give the items on your list the space to develop into worry and metastasise into anxiety that starts to cloud your view, stoop your shoulders, and shrink your world.

For now, use whatever medium you prefer—a notepad, your tablet, a notes app on your phone. You're also going to need a timer—a watch, stove timer, mobile phone app—whatever you like, so long as it can count down 5 minutes.

1. First, dig up whatever to do lists you already have. Come on, I know you have them.
2. Merge them all into this one. Add headings or dot points or whatever takes your fancy. Just get them in.
3. Next, while you're doing that, it's very likely other tasks will occur to you, things you've been meaning to do. Just write—get them in. Don't worry about double-ups, you'll sort that out later.
4. Sooner or later the well will start to run dry. Once that happens, think of the big projects that are sitting in the background that you've been meaning to do but haven't yet. Little tasks might still occur to you while doing that, get them down, too.
5. Pretty soon that well will also start to run dry. Ask yourself what might be missing that you would like to have in there, in various areas of your life. We're talking your money questions and bigger finance/future concerns, your health—both mental and physical—relationships with family and friends, hobbies and leisure activities, career or scholastic advancement. Keep writing as things occur to you.
6. Once you run out, it's time for the timer. Set it to count down from 5 minutes. Don't get up or start doing something else yet, scan your brain for anything else that needs to be added.
7. Do *not* get up until that timer goes off.
8. Here's the really tough bit: if you think of anything,

> write that down and restart the timer. The exercise is not complete until you hear crickets fully for five minutes.

Pause in your reading and go ahead to do this exercise now. You can pick the book back up when you're done.

The lightness of being

Congratulations. If you saw the process through without fudging, you've done an admirable job, I know that very well myself.

Take a moment now to sit and reflect on your list. How many line items is it? That's what was on your mind! Is it any wonder you've been feeling tense? How do you feel now that it's all on paper and you don't have to have it weighing you down? The sort of experience I'd expect you to be telling me about is a feeling of lightness, of peace, of inner quiet, even.

Okay, so there's one more part to the exercise, and when that's complete, whatever you're feeling now will double. The last step in this exercise is to decide which items are worth doing and get those ones into motion.

Don't panic. Not yet, anyway.

I realise that you most likely have many dozens of items on your list (and maybe many times that number). The purpose is not to get them all done yesterday, the purpose is to joyfully work through the ones that are important as part of your ongoing experience, and we're not going to do that today.

This is where your GPS will come into its own, as you'll see later in this book.

Ah ha's . . .

- *Whereas the principle of getting financially organised is the key to solving your financial unrest, the GPS is your guiding light, illuminating your pathway forward.*
- *Your GPS is also your go-to repository for all things future and all things financial, your 'safehouse'. Use it and nothing is missed and everything that needs to be dealt with will be dealt with, but not on-the-fly when you're doing something else or your resources are depleted—instead, you'll employ processes in your scheduled progress meetings that unpack this stuff and put it back together in ways that elevate you rather than depress or exhaust you.*
- *Using your GPS in this way sops up any worries or anxieties about unresolved money planning problems—current or future—and the quiet-but-heavy frustrations lurking in the back recesses of your mind which disrupt any chance you have of real peace.*

By the way . . .

If you're feeling somewhat swamped at this point—have questions because something doesn't make sense, or you need something extra before you dive into the Method—we're here to help. Book a chat with us on

www.danielbrammall.com/roadmap-page

Chapter 7

The Meat on the Bones

"Out of clutter, find simplicity."

—Albert Einstein

Having met the backbone (the GPS), it's time to meet the meat.

Sorry that was lame. But you're seven chapters in now, so I thought you could do with a smile.

Okay—*it's time for the BIG reveal of the Independent Planning-for-results Method* so you can see how you are going to execute on this framework to get the results you want.

Are your seatbelts on? There's a lot to cover this chapter, but in its essence the IP4R Method is simple and consists of three distinct phases.

Deep Planning—This phase exists to deliver you *compelling clarity* about your future.

Roadmap—The end-result of this phase is *crystal clear direction* from a solid plan.

Results—The fun part—visible proof of *tangible progress* towards your future.

These three phases operate together to deliver you the results you seek—replacing financial worries with confidence and certainty.

As tempted as you might be to rush forward, the counter-intuitive reality is that you get quicker and longer-lasting results when you execute these phases in sequence, one after the other. Yes, there's a bit to it, but it really is as simple as shampooing: 'lather, rinse and repeat'. It's a sure path to creating bulletproof finances.

As you execute each phase, you create specific tools that are used in subsequent steps of the process. These tools are your own valuable intellectual property assets because they help you generate a return on your investment of time and energy into the IP4R Method. Hardly surprising that you'd create assets in a book about transforming your financial future.

Building the assets is not a chore, it's actually enjoyable. Why? Because it's about all you hold dear, your own reasons for going to all this effort. These are the prerequisites to answering all the questions you had when you picked up this book in the first place.

Your assets grow into a portfolio, the portfolio delivers the returns you seek from your investment in this process. As you continue to execute, you build momentum, your Financial House progressively becomes more orderly and your confidence grows as you watch the future you intended begin to take shape.

Deep Planning—capturing a clear and compelling future

The purpose of this first phase, as you'd expect from its name, is to envision the future you want with the type of clarity that can make it real. You accomplish this in three steps:

1. Capture *your context.*
2. Reveal *your 'must-haves'.*
3. Track *your progress* from today's starting line.

In the context of your Financial House—that concept which will either support or confound your attempts to create the future you want—these three steps are the foundation on which your house will be built. They're your bigger picture, your reasons for making this investment of time and energy, and they're going to keep you on track when distractions seek to pull you off-course.

Capturing your context

As the anonymous quote goes: "*Find me a big enough 'why' and the 'how' will look after itself.*" The framework of this IP4R Method is the 'how', your job is to supply the 'why'.

To understand Deep Planning, let's go back a step . . .

The reason you're here today with this book in your hands is that you aren't where you want to be and there are lots of distractions, noise and obstacles preventing you from making progress in a meaningful way. There has to be a better way, and there is: by getting organised, you give yourself a much (MUCH!) higher probability that you will get to where you want to go.

So where do you want to go? What's the ultimate destination here?

Having an objective in mind is obviously a prerequisite before you set off, unless you want to end up going round and round in circles. It pays to reason, then, that we ought not to presume the first goal that occurs to us is the one we need to set as our big objective. Getting that objective right is a big deal.

For instance, a goal that is more like a whim is really a shiny bauble whose lustre soon fades. Whims steal your money and leave you feeling unsatisfied and disappointed. Likewise, a goal that is pure fantasy is like chasing a rainbow. Chasing rainbows robs you of your time, which is a resource in limited supply. In fact, considering it's the only resource you can't replace once it's spent, it's easily the most valuable, a fact that starts staring you in the face unpleasantly as you get older. Perhaps you had a glimpse of this nasty stare on your 40th, 50th,or 60th birthday.

A valued direction

So you see, then, the importance of setting your objective without whimsy and without fantasy. The best way to do that is to ensure your destination lies at the end of what the psychologists call your *'valued direction'*. Without getting hung up on new-age terms like 'values', your valued direction consists of a chain of concepts that you rank according to your own unique hierarchy. A 'value chain', if you will.

In classical economics, the 'value chain' is a process that takes an otherwise useless, raw material and, through a series of events, progressively improves it so that, by the end of the process, the raw material has been transformed into something valuable and useful.

In the same way, your personal value chain is what transforms a number of options or alternatives available to you—raw materials—into a clear and valuable choice that will serve your greater purposes. By clarifying your hierarchy of what's most important to you, you make it easier to make better decisions from all the options available and walk in a valued direction towards your objective.

Hence your goal is actually something you pursue while walking in a valued direction. It's the direction that's valued, the goal is the destination, but if you don't value the direction, then the walk to the goal is miserable. This, in turn, has a direct impact on how likely you are to follow through.

Beyond goals: uncovering your 'Must-Haves'

Recall that the reason for capturing your context is to set up a framework for powerful decisions supporting objectives that are meaningful and compelling to you. Objectives like these are more likely to appear in your future because they're not nice-to-haves, they're part of your fabric and are calling to you. They're part of who you are. We call them '*must-haves*'.

The danger of not having must-haves is that if you go through a goal setting process and arrive at a number of 'nice-to-haves' then—at the end of the day—that's just a 'wish list'. The future you want for you and your family isn't a wish list, that's not what I'm talking about. I'm talking about something that you need to have in your future like you need to take your next breath.

Next, who are you taking on your journey? You see, shaping your future usually isn't a solo exercise; there's you . . . and who else? How are these people connected to you? How do they need to factor into your planning?

Identifying who's close to you and clarifying their relationship to you is key here. These are folks whose welfare you are interested in or who are dependent on you in some way or another. You do that best by quickly sketching your own *Family Tree*.

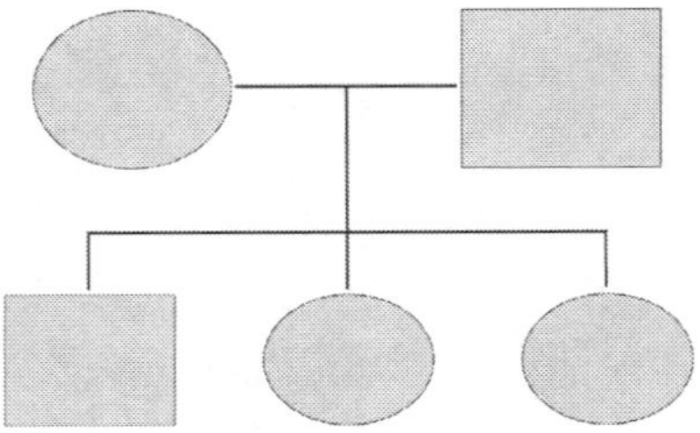

Your Family Tree is an asset you can easily get carried away with—because they're so cool. With just a few simple lines, circles and squares, family trees tell very human stories that span generations. So, to avoid over-investing in this exercise, remember the point of this asset: to capture the important parts for building on in the next exercise. It's not the intention to trace back your ancestry to its historical roots, although if that floats your boat, then once you're finished with this exercise, go for it.

I'll give you a very effective method to quickly capture your own Family Tree in Part 3 of this book.

It's time to add a third dimension to your context by combining your Must-Haves and your Family Tree into a timeline, called the *'Family Timeline'*, an asset giving you a unique perspective on where all this intersects in time, and how to best prepare for it all.

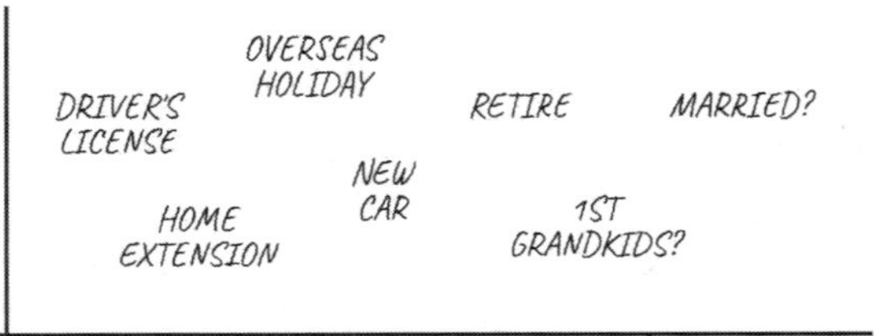

YEAR	2023	2028	2033	. . .
	50	55	60	. . .
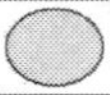	48	53	58	. . .
	15	20	25	. . .
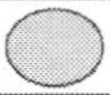	12	17	22	. . .
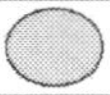	8	13	18	. . .

Every time I've facilitated this exercise for someone, probably without exception, I've heard them make the same observation; something similar to: "**gasp* our lives!*."

Confronting in a fun way, I'll show you how to do that soon. You're going to love this one because it captures some very significant parts of your entire life in one simple picture.

This asset gives you a very strong foundation to keep you rock solid as you move forward.

Now you're cooking. What's the plan?

Your Roadmap—a plan of action

The next logical step is to map out the route that will get you there in the shortest possible time, in the safest possible way. You can then simply follow your roadmap, step-by-step. In this, phase two of the Method, *you will establish your starting line, the finishing line, and a baseline*. This gives you a yardstick to measure how your finances are tracking as they evolve into bulletproof. It also helps you measure your progress along your valued direction towards your must-haves.

To establish the quickest, safest route, you're going to create assets that work together to illuminate the pathway forward and keep you from straying off that path. They'll quickly become part of your everyday life because they're your ticket to less worry and more certainty.

This starts with working out where you are with the next two assets, your *'Financial Snapshot'* and your *'Report Card'*. The Financial Snapshot is like your current coordinates on the map at any point in time, and the Report Card is like a status report of the car you're going to use to get to your destination—very important to know whether the car is in the sort of shape you need it to be in to take you where you want to go.

A financial snapshot

The 'cash is king' truism I spoke about earlier in this book starts to come to life in this exercise. Again, using the magical power of squares, circles and a few lines, this simple snapshot is going to give you more forward momentum every time you update it because it's a clear indicator of your return-on-investment from the Independent Planning-for-results Method.

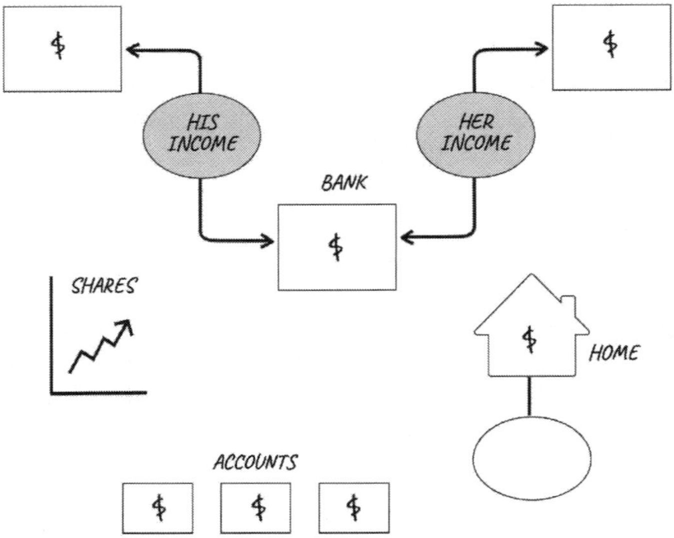

Assets are depicted by squares and liabilities by circles, and the flow of cash is shown by arrowed-lines that connect them.

Starting with the family's income, the cashflow chart shows how that money is channelled into retirement funds and working accounts. From there it is syphoned into various bank accounts and investments, and into debt repayments, such as the home loan.

The values for each asset and liability will change each time you update your cashflow chart (when you do this is something we'll come to in future chapters), as will the number of assets and liabilities on your chart.

One of the magical but subtle benefits of this simple chart is that not only is it an 'everything-in-one-glance' financial snapshot that your team can use and share to do their work for you (again, more on that later), but it's also a nice reminder of where your cash is supposed to go. Because each element on the chart has a purpose, the effect is you tend to think twice before you make deposits or withdrawals—should I be doing this, where should it be going to/coming from, what is that earmarked for?

The Financial Snapshot gives you a clearer picture of where you are today, so you have an even better idea of what's required to accomplish your must-haves. I spoke about the Report Card, but I'll come back to that in Phase 3. First, let's get some blueprints drawn up . . .

A blueprint for your must-haves

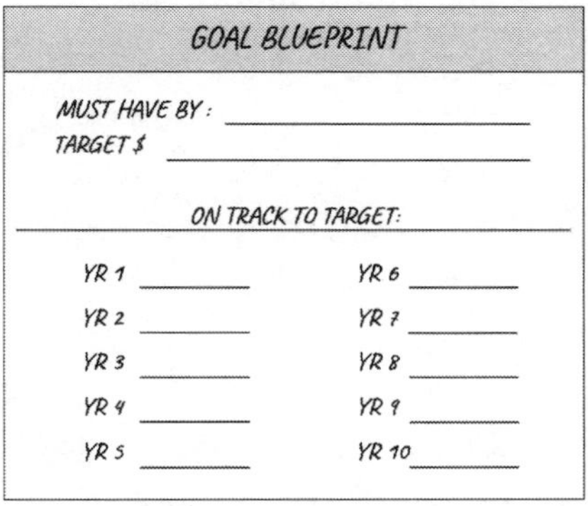

At its essence, a blueprint is a plan, schematic, drawing or other visual tool that shows you the details behind what it is you're trying to build, so you can build it.

Having captured your must-haves, you will develop a blueprint for each that shows the details of the funding plan, including where the money is going to come from, what the performance needs to be, and what 'on track' looks like at various forecast intervals on the road to the end result.

Having this asset in hand can give you an enormous sense of optimism and confidence you're going to accomplish your objectives because it brings them to life, each step of the way.

Pulling order out of chaos.

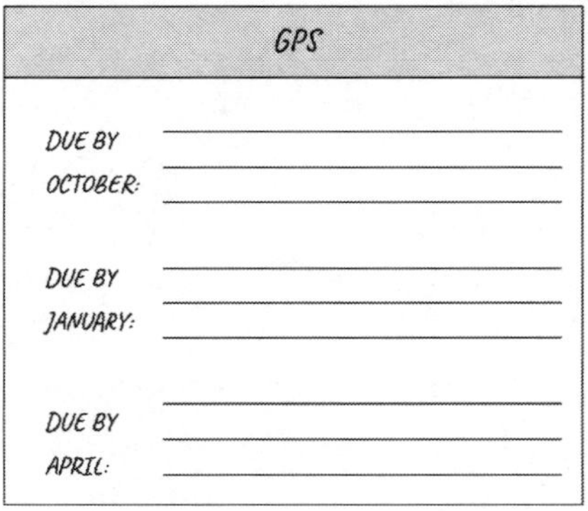

Your *Global Positioning System* is such an essential ingredient to turning down the noise so you can focus on (a) what's important to you, and (b) what's within your control. As a byproduct, you'll be able to see your desired results coming to fruition in the intended way.

Your GPS is your working plan of action that contains all the tasks that need to be done and when you need to have done them by so that your finances evolve into a bulletproof state.

For instance, your GPS will contain all the prescribed tasks that progress organising the rooms of your financial house that we covered in Chapter 4 (remember—the cash planning room, the wealth planning room, the tax planning room, and so on?). It also contains all due dates for your 'must haves' and for important milestones leading up to your must-haves, like those that are flagged in other assets such as your goal blueprint.

As we saw last chapter, the GPS is also the right place for you to download any 'ideas on the fly' that you want to include in the agenda for future progress meetings (a concept I'll describe in the next phase). This is your tool to defuse 3am ruminations so that they can be unpacked in a sensible way, at a sensible time, and a sensible solution developed.

Are you starting to see how this portfolio of assets works to fortify your financial house, support you through the noise and distractions, and ultimately and inexorably lead you towards the future you really desire?

The Results Phase—where the rubber meets the road

You now have a roadmap, a real plan consisting of multiple, interactive assets that are all action-oriented. This is not a plan of 'thinking'—all the thinking's already been done—it's a plan of action because *ultimately taking action is how you get a visible and tangible return on your investment.*

To make certain your roadmap translates into action, you are going to put a recurring meeting with yourself into your calendar. After all, a roadmap is only useful if you pick it up and look at it to see where you're at on it. Otherwise you might as well toss it out the window.

It's for this reason you hold *Progress Meetings*—it's the doing that brings you the results.

Rubber? Meet road.

Progress Meetings are the point at which the proverbial rubber hits the road.

The reality is that accomplishing something as important as bulletproofing your financial future and bringing all your must-haves into existence requires particular actions to be taken. This means there's a certain amount of work your must-haves require in order to be transformed from a mere idea into reality.

Progress Meetings are meetings with yourself, the purpose of which is to ensure the work has been done. These sessions are where you get to see the return on your investment into the IP4R Method. Each progress meeting has a target outcome and a specific agenda that has been designed to support that result.

Staying on-task

This term 'staying on-task' is not something I'd heard until I sat down for a parent-teacher interview about my oldest child, Laura. At the time, Laura was apparently having difficulty staying focussed on the subject at hand, and the teacher was having to continuously return to Laura's side to gently bring her back from wherever her attention had wandered to.

Meeting agendas are that gentle teacher. Having a well put together agenda is critical, as any company secretary will tell you. Without one, you can easily burn time you don't have, chasing rabbits down holes and getting distracted by largely irrelevant noise and other events beyond your control.

For this reason, each Progress Meeting has an agenda consisting of two main parts:

1. The regular business of every progress meeting;
2. Additional 'items on the fly' that have arisen since the last meeting and require some attention for progress to be made.

These meetings are called progress meetings for a reason—to appraise your progress. Here are the tools you use to do that.

Tracking your progress

In any area of life, we all know what it feels like when you're making zero progress.

If you've identified a valued direction that you want to head in and feel like you're spinning your wheels, frustration is your life. Worse, if it feels like you're going completely the wrong way, a feeling of hopelessness starts to creep in, and that can lead to outright depression.

On the other hand, when you're making progress towards a valued target then the air you breathe is sweet.

For most of the time that an aircraft is in the air, it's not pointing at its destination. However the pilot doesn't get frustrated or depressed because he or she relies on tools to track the aircraft's progress towards its target.

You need to know where you are, in two ways.

1. What sort of progress are you making towards your goal?
2. Are your finances evolving into a bulletproof condition?

Achieving your must-haves

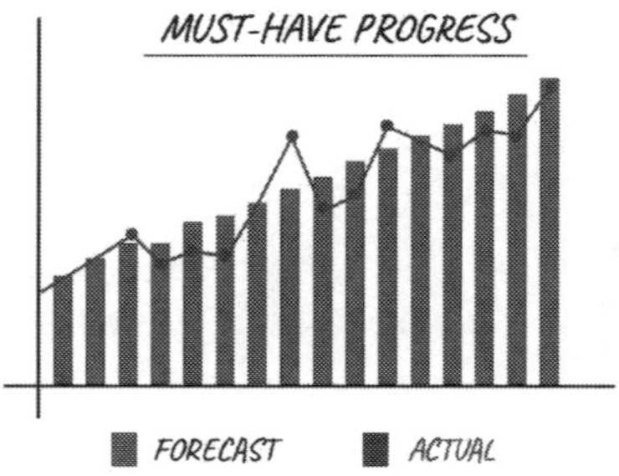

Having established your financial snapshot, and equipped also with a blueprint for each of your must-haves, you have all the ingredients you need to measure your progress towards your intended destination. *Progress Charts* are visual tools that represent the pinnacle of a lot of the work you've done to develop this portfolio of assets that you now own.

As the name might suggest, this very simple asset tells you in a single glance how you're progressing towards your must-haves. Visually, your progress charts do so much heavy lifting for you. They're a celebration, patting you on the back by showing you how far you've come. With each new progress update of your 'actual' and 'forecast', your momentum builds as the clear pathway in front of you inspires you to keep moving forward. If your 'actual' dips below the 'forecast' it is your gentle reminder to focus on what is within your control to get back on track, rather than obsess about external events that are hyped by the media.

As time goes by, a casual reflection on the journey you've experienced to arrive at your current update tells a story . . . you can easily see where your attention might have faltered because your actual dipped below forecast. Like the early warning system on a pilot's dashboard, your Progress Charts helps you avoid a costly trend that become increasingly difficult to correct. Looking at your journey to date also shows you where inevitable events beyond your control had an impact—market corrections and so on.

Your Progress Charts keep you rock solid through these times, impervious to events that are beyond your control. Events that used to cause you worry, increasing the risks of knee-jerk decisions to ward off anxiety, are now merely 'noise' . . . part and parcel of the process. For that reason alone your Goal Progress Charts are probably the most important and motivating asset in your entire portfolio.

Becoming financially bulletproof

You don't achieve goals every day; there are periods of activity in between goals. But there is another objective here, and that is to *make your finances bulletproof.* Remember that by doing this, you enhance your chances of achieving your goals. You also optimise your finances so that when events beyond your control—like the markets, the economy or world events—take a turn for the worse, you can keep your head about you when all others are losing theirs.

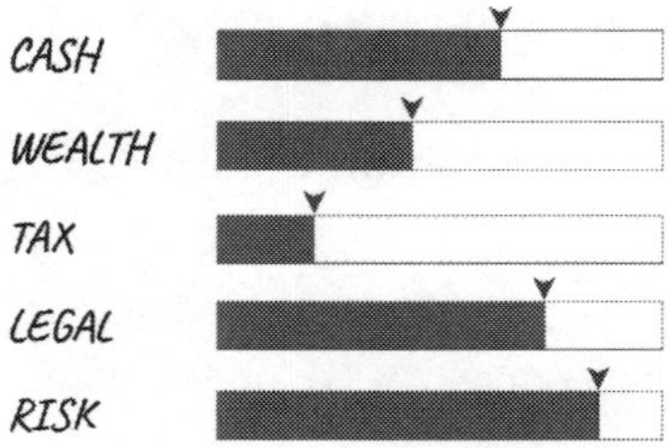

Your Report Card shows you how much headway you're making on that score.

This asset is inspired by the report card we used to get as

kids at school. At the end of each school term, our teacher handed us a (sealed) envelope that we would (usually) take home and give to mum and dad. This source of delight or misery basically told our parents how organised we were scholastically.

Your IP4RM Report Card gives you a quick and simple snapshot of how bulletproof your finances are at this point.

If it's not in your calendar, it won't happen

Schedule your progress meetings. If they're not in your calendar, then they're not likely to happen and the portfolio of assets you created in the previous two phases will start to wander aimlessly. So whether you use Google or Outlook or something else, these are recurring meetings with yourself (and your team, if you use one), scheduled in advance.

When you start out, set your progress meetings up for every three months. We call it the 90-day sprint. That's not so frequent as to be overwhelming and not so far apart as to lose sight of the goals or lose track of the action items.

As time goes by and you become progressively more organised, you can space things out a little more—obviously the more seasoned you are, the more organised you are, the less complex your situation will be, the more cohesive and coordinated your team will be, the more you can reduce the number to three or even two times a year.

At this point, some congratulations are appropriate. You've made it through the three main phases of the IP4RM method and seen how each component stacks on the previous one to progressively improve and optimise your finances, ultimately leading you to a certain, bulletproof future.

Changing gears . . .

Before we get into the 'doing' of Part 3 in this book, just in case you're feeling the pinch a little and wonder if there's a helping hand available somewhere: there totally is. Jump into the resources section at the back of this book for ideas on how to do that.

That said, we're going to change gears now because, in the

next chapter, you're going to find your own personal 'ground zero' for building the future you want. This is about clarifying your own *Valued Direction* which, for some, might sound like a soft, warm and fuzzy notion, I can assure you it's very firmly grounded in psychological science and will work very nicely if you give it the attention it deserves. It's also fun.

Ah ha's . . .

- *At its heart the* Independent Planning-for-results Method *is very simple. The key that makes the Method so effective is the concept of becoming financially organised. Getting your entire Financial House in order not only bulletproofs your finances, it gives you the highest probability of making your desired financial future a reality.*
- *The IP4RM delivers a transformation from financial anxiety and uncertainty to a state of confident certainty, in three distinct phases.*
    1. *The first phase of the Method starts with a process of Deep Planning to reveal a valued direction towards clear, must-have outcomes. Along the way you create valuable intellectual property assets, such as a Family Timeline, that will support and guide your progress.*
    2. *During the next phase, a number of additional assets are created to serve as your Roadmap. These tools, like the 'Must-Have Blueprint' and your 'GPS', work together to keep you on a clear path forward.*
    3. *The final phase is where the results come from. Using the assets of your Roadmap to lead the way, regular check-ins are scheduled, called Progress Meetings. These follow a set agenda designed to ensure nothing is left to chance and all the plan's action items are accounted for.*
- *Each step in the process builds on the last to lead you inexorably to a bulletproof financial future.*

Chapter 8

Towards a Valued Direction

"It takes something more than intelligence to act intelligently."
—Fyodor Dostoyevsky

As we've seen in the first part of this book, what prevents people from developing good plans is, by and large, the problem of being disorganised. The critical tool to combat disorganisation is your Global Positioning System, the backbone of the Method's three phases.

If you were to execute just on these simple concepts I've taught you in this book so far, that alone would cause you to experience less anxiety, more certainty and more momentum.

But this is only one part of what makes the IP4RM so effective.

If you imagine for a moment that the idea of getting organised is like the concept of an automobile that will take you where you want to go, if your GPS is the engine that drives that automobile, your Valued Direction is the fuel powering your engine.

Deep Planning is the process by which you reveal your Valued Direction, and so in this chapter I provide you the same planning exercise I facilitate for my clients to help them accomplish this[1]. Use the exercise to do the same for yourself.

---

[1] Not the inventor, but a huge fan and avid practitioner. I've tried to trace this idea back to its source, but it seems I'm not the only fan and there have been many contributors to this idea over the years. Probably the best exponent I've ever met is Bill Bachrach, author of *Values Based Financial Planning*.

Your Value Chain

The heart of your valued direction, your *Value Chain* is an enduring asset whose worth will show up again and again as you continue making choices about your finances that shape your future. When it comes down to it, making smart choices is the name of the game here. The Independent Planning-for-results Method is built on that concept.

Making smart decisions, though, doesn't only happen in relaxing and inviting environments . . . very often we need to make a really good decision in those clutch moments, when the stakes are high and the pressure is on and the odds are stacked against us.

That's why it's valuable beyond measure to clearly establish what is going to constitute a good decision for you as an individual, considering your bigger context, because it's different for all of us. This is what your Value Chain is so useful for—it clarifies what's truly important to *you*. In a nutshell, the values on which our decisions are based determine whether we feel good or bad about those decisions.

There's a story about an elderly statesman that illustrates this beautifully . . .

The elderly statesman

This particular guy built a fantastic business over 70 years ago that continues to delight its customers even to this day. His business has become a household name globally and people travel from all over the world—and bring their kids—just to experience it.

He started it from scratch together with his brother who had an idea one day while watching his two daughters ride a merry-go-round. A productively employed banker who was recovering from tuberculosis, he nonetheless threw his lot in with his brother who was, at the time, a formerly-broke cartoonist. He put it all on the line to follow the dream.

In the afterglow of his now-successful business, a fascinated journalist who had heard the rag-to-riches story of how he threw himself completely into this fantasy of a future that had been conjured up in someone else's head, asked him, "*How on earth did you keep up your momentum in spite of all the obstacles and just keep moving forward in the face of all this adversity that you overcame?.*"

His response was simple, "*When your values are clear to you, making decisions becomes easier.*"

This is the guy who built Disneyland.

> *"The clearer you are about what is important to you, the better choices you'll make about what to do with your time."*
>
> **—Bill Bachrach**

The search for meaning

Don't worry, I'm not about to get all existential on you here. But at this point some context for your motivations about organising your finances is in order, particularly in light of the exercise I'm about to outline in this chapter. Let me explain why.

We all have the same amount of time given to us in a week: 168 hours for each of us. What you do with that time determines the quality of your life. For instance, if you spend your time doing activities that have meaning for you, then your experience of that time is fulfilling. By comparison, if you spend your time doing tasks that are meaningless, your experience of that time is painful.

This is true even if it's accurate to say that you spent that time striving and struggling. To endure discomfort and difficulty while striving for something meaningful and worthwhile is a freely chosen, rewarding task.

Ask any parent standing in the freezing cold early on a Saturday morning, cheering encouragement to their child from the sideline of a soccer game. Consider another scenario: spending the same morning freezing your butt off on the side of the road because your car broke down on the way to the soccer game which you completely missed . . . not a rewarding struggle.

The clearer you can get about what's important, the better choices you'll make. This is particularly true when it comes to money. With that in mind, let's get started . . .

Capturing your value chain

If you can't set yourself aside 20 minutes right now for the exercise I'm about to show you, that's fine, go ahead and keep reading for now so you get an idea of what it's about. Consider making a reminder to return to this exercise later when you can give it your full attention because it has the potential to be a valuable experience.

It's actually best done as a facilitated exercise rather than on your own, and the more times your facilitator has done this, obviously the better the experience will be for you. So, if you can, grab a partner (can be your spouse or someone else you can trust). If you're flying solo, though, that's okay for now. I'm going to give you directions on how to conduct the exercise with a partner, but you can roleplay if you are alone.

In the resources section at the end of this book you'll find a link to the bonuses that came with this book, including a workbook with all the templates, one being the Value Chain illustration you see to the right.

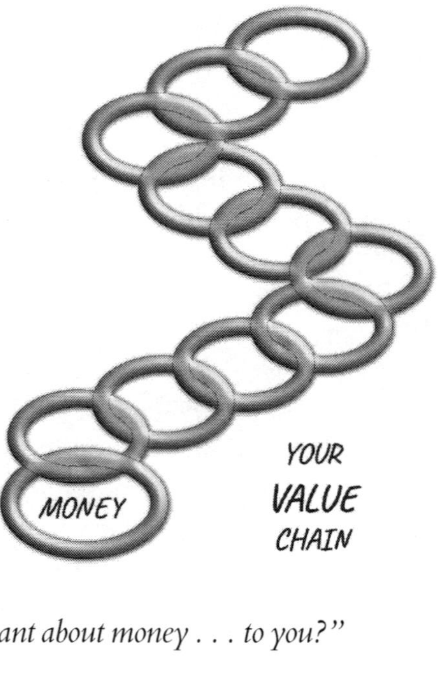

First, write their name underneath and, on the first step immediately above their name, write the word "money." Now put the pen down, turn the page around so they can see it, pause, and ask the following question:

"(Name), what's important about money . . . to you?"

Now shut up. Just wait until they're finished, and I mean completely finished. Don't touch that pen! Leave it there and wait until they're done. Keep a 'neutral' disposition about yourself—you're not here to judge or rate their answers, you're here to listen while their internal dialogue processes the question. Sure, you can give a few nods while they're speaking, but don't interject or agree/disagree or add your own comments. Keep a neutral visage and just wait to make sure they've answered the question as fully as they know how.

If you're doing this exercise solo then you need to stick to the rules to get the most from it. It might feel weird but the chances are excellent you do weirder things when unobserved! Ask yourself the question aloud and work at it until you have fully explored the question.

This question is likely to draw anything from blank looks to a verbal 'stream of consciousness' that lasts minutes. What's really happening is they are reflecting on what is, after all, a question that we assume has a simple answer. It doesn't. It has an answer that is deceptively deep; continuing to consider it can yield profound discoveries that will genuinely help set you on the path to smart decisions that are smart *for you*.

As they answer the question, whether there are long pauses or non-stop monologue, don't prompt them and, as tempting as it is, don't attempt to finish their sentences. This is stream of consciousness stuff. Also, avoid the temptation to fill in any uncomfortable silences with banter or your own observations. Be genuinely neutral and just be 100% attentive, listening intently to their response. Don't pick up that pen till it's clear they're absolutely finished.

In any event, when they're done, you can pick the pen back up and turn the page round to face yourself so you can write on it.

Your task now, having listened intently to every single word they said, is to pick out a word or phrase they said which sums up their stream of consciousness. Don't paraphrase, don't add words that weren't said. It's important to capture the essence of what's important about money to them using words that were actually said and are therefore meaningful to them. At the same time, you don't want to transcribe every word that was uttered. There's likely to be a phrase or a few words they used which effectively sum up the whole monologue—*that's* what you write down.

Confirm that the words you write capture the essence of what they said, being careful not to use words they didn't utter. Remember, their words have meaning for them, use their words, not yours. Now, putting the pen down, turn the page around again to face them, and, looking them in the eye, ask you your second tough question of the day:

> *"(Name), what's important about (your last answer) . . . to you?"*

Again, you're likely to get anything from more blank stares . . . to *War and Peace*. Don't be put off by the blank stares. They're actually not staring at you, they're thinking. They probably can't even see you, such is their internal dialogue.

Whatever their reply, resist the temptation to help them. They can do this without help if given a little space for thought. Your job is to listen and really, really hear them.

Humans have a deep and abiding need to be really heard. Turning off your internal dialogue, being 100% involved and present, and genuinely, truly listening intently to what someone is saying is a priceless skill. Developing it into a habit will do more to deepen your understanding of the human condition than any other single thing. It'll also make you the most popular person in the room at any party.

Once they've finished their answer, turn the page around, pick up the pen and write the new answer, as before, on the step above their last response. Confirm with them that you got it right. Then, with the pen down, turn the roadmap around so they can see your response, and go again.

As they continue to explore this territory they're likely to have a few 'ah ha' moments. Although what we each get from this exercise is different, there does tend to be a pattern when it is executed properly . . .

Their first answer is likely to be about basic things that money delivers you. Words you might hear are often things like "security", "freedom", "time", or "independence." These are generally basic needs we all have, intangibles that money needs to do for us. Whatever was said is what works for them.

As you work with the exercise, if you have been listening with keen, non-judgmental interest, it's likely your partner's responses will move from the basic needs that money fulfils for them, and head towards an even bigger picture—the things that are important to them at a deeper level.

Now that money is out of the way, they are free to consider other, higher values. Generally this is something beyond their own needs, we're looking outwards, usually at something to do with others. You might hear talk about the environment, charitable causes, their children, the community.

This type of answer might sound like this . . .

"I want to contribute to others."

"Helping the kids have great experiences."

"Giving back to the community."

"Securing a better future for the planet."

They are on their way to 'purpose' stuff, 'why I'm here' stuff. They are beginning to define their 'why'.

Repeat the question "*What's important about (your last answer) . . . to you?*"

Stay in the moment and non-judgemental—neither approving or disapproving. Simply listen.

Their responses might have filled up the Value Chain, they might not. Once they progress through these 'external/for others' type answers, they may start to talk in terms of how it will feel for them to have fulfilled those values.

You might hear this summed up something like "*Because that's what life's all about, isn't it?*" or "*That's why I'm here.*"

Other things that might come up are terms like 'fulfillment', 'a sense of satisfaction', 'peace', 'ultimate achievement' or 'self actualisation'. There might be long pauses. There might even be a few tears.

Wherever it goes is fine. There's no right or wrong answer. There's no goal or target point to achieve in order to say you've done it right.

You'll know when they've got to the end of their Value Chain, though, when they run out of answers.

What you have now is a Value Chain that is complete: a list of those things that are most important to you after the money issue is taken care of. These are their reasons, and when you take your turn, your answers will be your reasons.

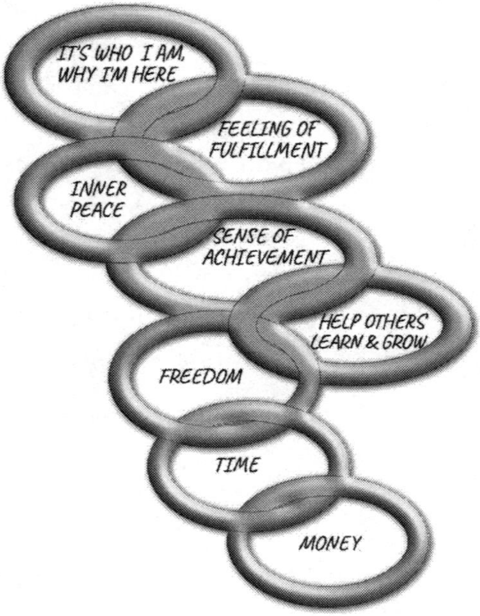

When you connect the links of your Value Chain into one simple statement, you get your own 'juice of life', giving you clarity and direction. The Chain above, for example, sounds like this:

> *"I'd like to have a plan for my money that gives me time so I can be free to help others learn and grow and have a sense of achievement which will bring me inner peace, and a feeling of fulfilment, because ultimately, that's who I am, that's why I'm here."*

It's your framework for evaluating whether a financial decision is right for you. From this day forward you can ignore what the talking heads on TV say or what the brother-in-law and all the other experts say is the right thing to do.

From now, when considering a financial decision, refer back

to your value chain. Does it have a positive or negative or neutral impact on what you say matters to you? Does it free up your time to experience more of what's important to you?

> *"There is more to see than can ever be seen,*
> *more to do than can ever be done."*
>
> —**Elton John,** *Circle of Life*

How and why this works

Touchy feely? Sure. A waste of time? Nope. Absolutely nope.

Trust me: in many years of helping folks make decisions about their finances and planning their future, getting the context clear—taking a moment to work out what makes you tick before you wind the clock—is a whole lot more effective than simply racing forward like a bull at a gate.

I've chosen not to get bogged down in the science of why this stuff works. Yes, the science behind it is well researched—you could start by Googling '*Maslow's hierarchy of needs*', which he wrote in 1954 (and he wasn't the first)—but even knowing the science back to front doesn't help you as much as just doing the exercise. You could do worse, too, than read Viktor Frankl's thoughts on the value of clarity about what's important; he shares his experiences surviving the concentration camps of Nazi Germany in *Man's Search for Meaning (1946)*.

Some of us prefer not to get into this fluffy stuff and others ache for it. We're all different. However, the truth is this: we've all got blood pumping through our veins. That's why this works.

I guess that's what I find so resonant about Elton John's quote, above—if you don't get clear on what matters, you're going to waste a lot of your life chasing shiny objects. And there's no shortage of them, as we all know. So take a moment to dig deep into what's important, truly important, to you so that you can be super clear on where you're going to get your 'marrow of life'.

Why good plans still fail

One of the most common reasons a good plan fails to come to fruition is because it lacked a valued direction and simply ran out of gas. Died on the vine, so to speak.

Poor planning like this leads to 'meh' objectives. Uninspiring goals take you nowhere.

Having a valued direction captured in your own value chain makes your plan much more likely to succeed, as you're about to see in the next chapter, which means you're well on your way to optimised finances and a bulletproof future.

Ah ha's . . .

- *Getting your Financial House in perfect order forever is what's going to take you where you want to go—it's the automobile you will drive to your destination, a place called 'Bulletproof-Future Town'.*
- *If your GPS is the engine, keeping you moving forward on your journey, then your Valued Direction is the fuel providing the power for the entire car. Without it the journey won't last very long.*
- *The asset at the heart of your Valued Direction is your Value Chain, a framework for keeping you grounded in your context as you make important decisions, especially financial ones.*
- *Having clarity on what's most important also does the groundwork for setting objectives that are meaningful and inspiring to you.*

Part 3

The Lowest Hanging Fruit

The remainder of this book is devoted to executing on this Method so you can bulletproof your financial future.

Chapter 9

Revealing Your Must-Haves

"The best way to predict the future is to invent it."
—Alan Kay

Last chapter, I used an automobile analogy to bring some perspective to the various assets of this Method that you've seen so far. To round out that analogy considering this chapter's purpose . . .

- The *destination* you'd like to reach is less worry and more confidence about your finances so you have a more certain future.
- The principle of getting your *Financial House* in order is like the car that will get you to that destination.
- Your *GPS* is the engine that drives your car forward.
- If your *Valued Direction* is the fuel powering that engine, then . . .
- Your *Must-Haves* are your steering-wheel.

You use the steering wheel to stay in your lane and to swerve to avoid the deer. Your Must-Haves serve another purpose, as valuable milestones that signify you're on the right track and making progress to your journey. They're your stepping stone objectives along the way to your ultimate destination, 'Bulletproof-Future Town'.

From wishes to goals

We all wish for stuff. Personally, I'd like a six pack and a Maserati. By when, though?

Ah. Put a date on it and it has a different feeling.

There are three big differences between a goal and a wish. Whereas a wish is something we want, a goal is something we want expressed in terms that are:

- Specific,
- Time-bounded, and
- Measurable.

Building on the clarity you obtained in the last chapter by *capturing your own valued direction*, you're now prepared to identify the 'Milestones of Progress' that you want to have happen in your future. Achieving these milestones is the fun part that proves you're *actually* making progress.

Often we'll have an idea of the direction we want to head in and roughly what we want, but aiming at blurry goals consigns you to never really being satisfied and always wondering whether you've hit the mark. In fact, without crystal clear clarity about what you want to accomplish, it's hard to even know if you're on target.

Been there, done that, got the t-shirt?

"Is this about goal setting?"

"I've already been to a hundred goal setting workshops."

"I'll skip this chapter."

There are only two reasons why you'd ever attend more than one goal setting workshop—either you failed to achieve your goal, which is frustrating—or you did achieve it and felt empty afterwards, which is depressing. Take heart because this chapter is the last 'workshop' you'll need to attend.

"I'm retired. I don't have any goals."

I've heard that a few times, actually. One of the reasons retirees can struggle with goals is they're seen to be something you accomplish in the distant future, therefore the incorrect conclusion is that there are no goals left to achieve. To get past this mental roadblock, the conversation often sounds like this . . .

Retiree: "*Look, I just want advice on choosing the right pension fund. I've researched it all and boiled it down to three.*"

Adviser: "*No problem. What do you want the pension fund to do for you?*"

Retiree: "*What do you mean? I want it to pay a pension, not take too many risks so it holds its value, and be accessible in case I want it to buy something extra.*"

Adviser: "*Okay. How much do you want it to pay you as a pension, starting when, and for how long?*"

Retiree: "*I want ten thousand a month, and I want it for—I dunno—forever, I guess.*"

This retiree thought she wanted advice to choose a pension fund. The underlying assumption is that she believed a pension fund was the best available option to get a regular, secure retirement income. As a result she'd become fixated on finding that needle in the haystack: the best pension fund.

The reality is that she didn't want a pension fund at all. What she wanted was a secure way to receive $10k a month forever. She'd lost sight of her objective on the horizon because her gaze was locked on all the boats at the dock—they all look the same, which one should I get in?

There might have been a luxury yacht around the corner leaving in twenty minutes, with vacant rooms they're almost giving away. She wouldn't have seen it because of her closed mind.

By setting her sights on the outcome, she opens up a world of possibilities. Her new goal is: "*I want the highest possible certainty of $10k per month, for life, starting now.*"

From goals to Must-Haves

One of the biggest pitfalls in goal-setting is 'meh' goals. They take you nowhere. If these characteristics feature in your goals, then they're meh. Meh goals have these features . . .

They're short term.

When we talk about planning your future, we're not talking about where you're going for lunch tomorrow, we're talking about your bigger picture. Set goals that take you to your horizon, not to your next footfall.

They're vague.

Is your goal so detailed, so specific that you can almost taste it? We're not talking about nothing-but-perfection here. Just be clear so you know where you're aiming.

They're easy.

Will accomplishing this goal be a stretch and demand at least your concerted effort to achieve it, or will it be a walk in the park? If it doesn't feel at least a bit unattainable, then think bigger. If you feel a little apprehensive or even daunted at the prospect, and a huge sigh of relief and excitement when you think about accomplishing it, you're on the right track.

They're not compelling.

How much do you want it? When you think about your goal, does it inspire and motivate you to take action? Does it give you the 'eye of the tiger'? Are you dead-serious about it?

Goals that are the opposite aren't merely goals anymore, they're '**Must-Haves**'. They look more like this:

They're longer-term.

Must-Haves are part of your bigger picture, they play a more important role in your future.

They're very (very!) specific.

You know what it is and when it is, down to the day. If you don't know where the goalposts are then which way do you kick the ball?

They're a stretch.

In our financial context we're talking about a tangible goal that requires money and planning to achieve it. It's going to take something of you to accomplish this thing. After all, if it's a foregone conclusion and requires no effort, is it something that's really going to be an achievement?

They're very (very!) compelling.

Not only do you know what it is and when it is, you know what it's going to feel like when you're there.

Whims and fantasies

Ever been to an Amway "event"? Greg, a friend of mine, dragged me along to one once. During the event, I saw that the company had taught him about goal setting and how multi-level marketing could help him create the money to achieve these goals. They encouraged him to think big. Obscenely big, as it happens.

Greg had pasted cut-out pictures onto a huge collage on his wall with target dates. A mansion with 20 rooms on huge acreage, a red Ferrari, the best select schools for his many children, lavish holidays to exotic locations, jewellery, and so on. Greg had actually done a great job of being as clear and specific as possible about what he wanted, and when he wanted it.

Why, then, did he fail to reach these goals? Think of it this way:

fantasies and whims → 'meh' goals →
frustration, cynicism, depression

versus

a meaningful and valued direction → must-haves →
purpose and peace

Greg's goals lacked meaning. They were lovely whims to fantasise about, like looking at your Rolls Royce parked under the 20-room mansion on a hill overlooking your private beach, while you sit back counting a million a year in royalties. They were indulgences of Greg's ego, not what really moves him as a father, as a son, as an entrepreneur, as a member of his community, as a resident on the planet.

Great things can be accomplished when you connect what you want with powerful reasons why. When you forget your why, you lose your driving force and stop consistently doing the work your goals require to achieve them.

Bringing your future to life—a practical exercise

How many times have you heard your mother say "if I won the Lottery all our problems would be over"?

We tend to fixate on this thing called money but it really has no meaning in and of itself. It's actually just a social system of value exchange. Money enables us to swap something of socially agreed value for something else we value. Economics 101.

What this means is that money's not as important as other things we swap money for, the things we simply must have. *The challenge, then, is to identify those Must-Haves using your Valued Direction to guide the way.*

To set the scene, pull out your completed Values Chain from last chapter. Running your hand from the bottom to the top, just reflect for a moment on what's important to you, linking each value together. For instance, let me share an example Value Chain with you. It looks like this:

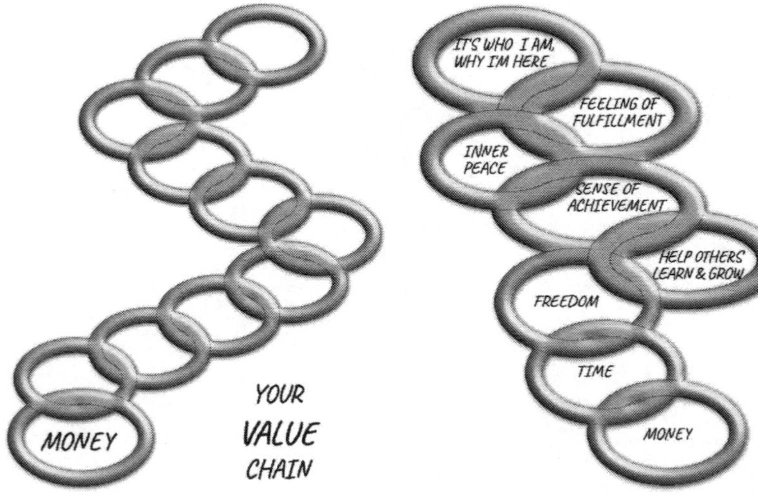

These are the qualities I value highly and, when strung together into a concise sentence or two, for me effectively become a very compelling mission statement, of sorts. It sounds like this:

> *"What's important about money to me is, firstly, that it gives me time. And having that time really gives me a sense of freedom which, in turn, makes me feel independent. Being independent means I am able to help others learn and grow, which then gives me a sense of achievement and, ultimately, a real feeling of inner peace and fulfilment. Because that's who I am, that's why I'm here."*

With that context in mind, I'm well placed to design myself a future worth living.

Making your future visible and vivid

In the context of your values—what's most meaningful and important to you—it's time to reveal your *Must-Haves*. Like the value chain exercise from last chapter, this exercise can be facilitated solo or with a partner (more fun and often easier with a partner).

There are rumours of studies verifying that having written goals massively increases the likelihood of achieving them. I'm not going to get into that—all I can tell you is that I've been through this process with many, many people. And more often than not when I ask what they found the most valuable about the exercise they just completed, they say that something in their heads shifted a gear when they saw it written down in specific terms. They took ownership, and that's a key to making your Must-Haves a reality.

In the light of 'high-definition resolution' and clarity about what's meaningful and important to you, here's a useful question to ask:

> *"What's a significant, worthwhile goal that will require money and planning to achieve? More than that—what is it that you* ***must have*** *in your future, beyond a shadow of a doubt. It's* ***not*** *optional."*

We're not talking about a new fridge. Sure, it might be overdue but it's not significant in the context of your valued direction. We're also not talking about losing five pounds, which might actually be a good idea but isn't going to require money to achieve it.

Here are some examples that come up again and again. Are any important to you?

Making work optional some day: "*I want to choose to work, not be forced to work. THEN I can do what's really been calling to me all these years.*"
Get the kids the best education: "*I want them to have a better start than the one I got, so they can choose their path.*"
Own a holiday home: "*So we connect as a family even when the kids are grown up and go and live their own lives, they'll still want to come . . . with their children too.*"
Take 3 months off work and travel around the country: "*No pressures, no deadlines. Just me, my spouse, and the open road.*"
Set up a charitable foundation for disadvantaged kids: "*It's because of something I experienced years ago when I was in Sri Lanka, it's stuck with me and I promised myself I'd do something about that.*"

Is there a stand-out in that list that you find compelling and meaningful? Perhaps it's something you can't see on the list, but it's been sitting in the dark recesses of your mind for years, and the idea has always taken your breath away if only you one day had the time and opportunity to drag it out into the sunlight?

Again—we're not talking about goal setting here. We're way beyond that. We are talking about a valued direction that results in bringing this Must-Have out of your imagined future and into your world as reality.

Okay, let's give that a name. What name would you give that Must-Have? Something meaningful to you. Don't overthink this—just use a word or a phrase that conjures up the image of achieving this Must-Have, one that's meaningful to you. For instance, if retirement is important but the word 'retirement' doesn't do it for you, then what about 'making work optional'?

If you're inclined to take out a pen and piece of paper rather than just read along, be my guest. You can use the format below which is a 'Must-Haves' worksheet. As a reminder, you'll find links to all these worksheets in the resources section at the end of this book.

My Must-Haves	
Name:	
Due Date:	
Target Sum:	
Think and Feel	

Now where were we? Your Must-Have: give it a name.

Got it?

If you did, nicely done. For what it's worth, when I'm doing this exercise with a client of mine, then whatever they write down on the paper is also a Must-Have for me and my team. It's ours as much as it is theirs. Powerful stuff.

But hey, for the purposes of this chapter, if the mood didn't strike you as you were reading this and you've not pulled out a piece of paper, no problem. There's no law against coming back to this later when the impulse strikes you. Let's keep moving forward, shall we?

Okay now we're going to get some really high resolution clarity about this, to do justice to the name of Must-Have. That means specific. I mean really specific. 'Imagine-it's-happening-tomorrow'-type specific.

Making work optional? By when? Not just the year. Insert a date. And how much will you need to live on?

Retiring in luxury—where to? What house will you live in? What car will you drive? What does 'retiring in luxury' look like to you, practically speaking?

The holiday home—how many bedrooms? What sort of kitchen? What features are important—a plunge pool? A rock-in' entertainment area? Home theatre? Pool table? Is it close to the beach? In the mountains? A sexy apartment in the heart of the city?

The holiday around the country—how much will it cost, including fuel, living money, a 4wd and a caravan? If you're not going to keep the caravan afterwards, what likely resale value will they have?

What are the best times of year to get to the tropics while still avoiding the tropical wet season? Will you need special gear like a rooftop tent or a satellite phone? How much time would be ideal to lazily wander back down the coast roads?

Now that you've had a moment to think about it from a different perspective . . .

By when?

Ask yourself: when do you want to have it by? Think about this in the context of the rest of your life.

If you have kids or other dependents, what age will they be in the year you achieve the objective? How old will you be? Does this date make sense from a broader perspective of your life? Choose the date you'd like to achieve this outcome—don't stop at simply choosing a year. You want a day to aim at. Write down the specific date that works best for you.

How much?

This is a piece of future that you want to take out of your imagination and make a part of your experience of living. It will require planning and money. How much money is it going to cost? Don't worry about inflation or growth or anything like that at the moment. For now, you want the figure in today's dollars.

For example, if your goal is called "Doing a Lap", which is shorthand for taking the whole family on a three month 4wd trip around the country, then you might work it out as follows:

Goal #1 (Trip Around Australia)	Cost
4wd (2nd hand, no resale afterwards - let's keep it!)	$40,000
Camper trailer (ditto)	$10,000
Equipment (bedding, cooking, fridge, etc.	$5,000
Fuel (13 weeks at $200 a week)	$2,600
Food (13 weeks at $100 a day, includes eating out)	$1,300
Spending (13 weeks at $50 a day)	$4,550
Contingency (10% of total)	$6,500
Total	$70,000

Let's try a different example. What about one that requires periodic income like retirement. Don't worry about the maths of what lump sum you're going to need, we'll do that later. Instead, just give some thought to how much you are going to need, net and spendable after tax, every month, to live the sort of retirement you want. It might look something like this:

Goal #2 (Retirement)	Cost per month
Cost of our current lifestyle now	$8,000
Less	
Mortgage (it'll be paid off)	$2,000
Kids (childcare/education/etc)	$2,000
Subtotal	$4,000
Plus	
Car upgrade every 5 years ($30K net cost = $6K per annum)	$500
Holidays (budget of $18K a year)	$1,500
Total	$6,000

This worked for the retiree I spoke of earlier in this chapter, whose Must-Have is to have $10k a month of net, spendable income for as long as she is likely to live, starting now.

Whatever your figure is, write it down.

Connecting your present reality

Recap: you're committed to this. This is something that is not a nice-to-have, it's a Must-Have. Whole different level. Failure is not an option.

It has a name, a financially enabling quantum, and a 'due by' date. What you're about to do is bring this into your present reality. I love this bit.

What is it going to feel like to have achieved that goal? Try this . . .

"Imagine you're there. It's <insert date here> and you have worked diligently towards this since <insert today's date here>. You've now got that money set aside and your Must-Have is accomplished. What are two or three words that describe what you're thinking and feeling, now that you've achieved your goal?"

Placing yourself into that future reality. What's it feel like? What emotions come up for you?

Do you heave a sigh of relief? Write that down: 'Relief!' You might feel like you've really achieved something worthwhile, you might feel proud—write that down. Whatever emotion you feel is what you want to nail down by writing it in the space provided.

This part of the exercise actually places you in the emotional position of having already achieved the Must-Have, which is why you talk about it in the present tense, as though it's now real. I'll spare you the psycho-babble, but suffice it to say that by imagining it first, the nervous system makes a neural (read: "emotional") connection between today's self image (your 'where you are today' identity) and the imagined one (your future 'where you want to be' identity). At least, that's what the behavioural psychologists tell us.

Either way, when we get to this part of the exercise, I see

people's body language change and their faces light up. So the message is: don't skip this bit.

Let's take a look at what a completed Must-Haves worksheet looks like using the example taken from above, "Doing a Lap."

My Must-Haves	
Name:	Doing a Lap
Due Date:	25 December 2030
Target Sum:	$100,000
Think and Feel	
Awesome. Connected. A good parent.	

Anchor it

Spend a moment now connecting this Must-Have to your future.

What's happening in other areas of your life now that you've accomplished your objective?

What's different?

What will you see, hear, feel, smell, taste?

What effect will this have on other areas of your life, other people in your life?

Where could you be?

This 'anchors' your Must-Have into your future context. We'll do more on the anchoring side of things later in this book using a tool called The Family Timeline. Once you've anchored, consider whether you have other Must-Haves that want to reveal themselves to you. Does anything leap out when you ask that question again?

> *"What's a significant, worthwhile goal that will require money and planning to achieve? More than that—what is it that you MUST HAVE in your future, beyond a shadow of a doubt? It's NOT optional."*

If nothing comes up right now, that's okay, you're done for the time being. If there is something more, though, then repeat the exercise. Take as much time as you want with this but just make sure you keep moving forward to the next chapter—it's important you keep your momentum going, and you can come back to this exercise as often as you like.

As a matter of fact, I'm willing to bet everything in my pocket that—when you've had the experience of seeing just how remarkably powerful this Must-Have asset is in delivering certain results about your future plans—you'll be back. And good for you, too.

Ah ha's . . .

- *Bulletproofing your finances makes the financial future you want more certain. To design that future, you use your Value Chain to reveal the Must-Haves you need in your life.*
- *Your Must-Haves are clear signposts telling you that you're making progress on your valued direction towards a bulletproof financial future.*
- *A must-have possesses four qualities that elevate it beyond a mere goal into something you simply have to have in your future. Not having it is not an option. You use those qualities to 'anchor' them to your future so you can bring them to life.*

Want help?

That was a lot of information to digest. Feeling overwhelmed? Consider yourself human. If you have questions or need clarity on something we have covered, my team is here to help.

To chat with my amazing team, visit:

www.danielbrammall.com/roadmap-page

Chapter 10

Adding Another Dimension

"Most difficult problems become very easy when we learn how to put things into perspective."
—Debasish Mridha

Okay, that was a lot to unpack.

It would be understandable if you're feeling a bit daunted about the sheer scale of executing on all these elements. At this point, it might be tempting to let overwhelm hijack your momentum and divert you down a rabbit hole. If you have a creeping sense that this is going to take forever, then just pause for a second, because it's not.

There's nothing better than scoring a goal early in the game. It really takes the pressure off and gives you momentum, something to build on.

If the last chapter left you a bit punch drunk, this chapter is going to breathe new life into your resolve and get you back in the game to really kick goals. You're about to take a quick shortcut so executing on the rest of the Method will be a breeze.

Who are you taking with you?

One of the biggest reasons more people don't have a financial plan to get themselves organised and bulletproof is because they don't know where to start. The best place to start is with this simple exercise whose purpose is to identify who needs to be included in your planning and doing.

This asset is called a *Family Tree*, and it works like this . . .

(By the way, a final reminder: all the blank templates you

need can be found in the resources section at the end of this book.)

It starts with a blank piece of paper or, if you do drawings and scribbles with a tablet, one of those. Pictured here is what a blank page looks like, in case you've forgotten. As a writer, I haven't; we hate them.

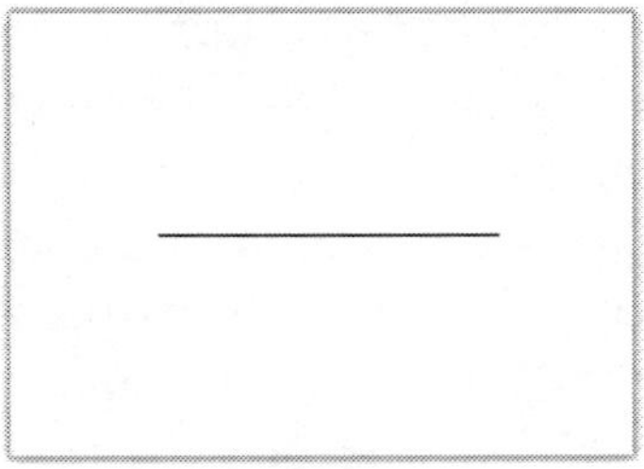

The first step in drawing up your Family Tree is—roughly in the centre of the page—to draw a horizontal line; not very wide, perhaps spanning no more than a quarter of the page. Like so . . .

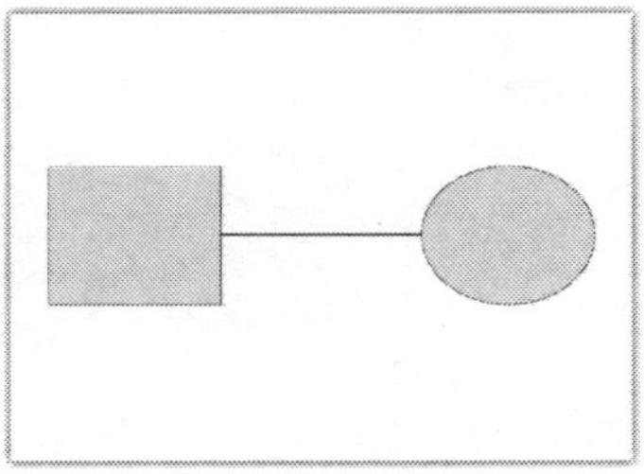

On each end of the line draw a circle or a square; a circle signifies female and square signifies male. One of these shapes represents you, the other represents your spouse. The line connecting the spouses signifies a relationship between the two shapes. By way of example, this diagram tells a story: it says that a male and a female are in a legal relationship (marriage, in this case).

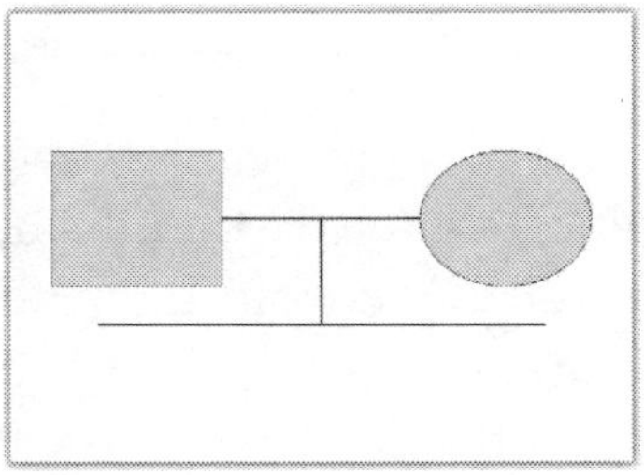

From the centrepoint of the line connecting the two shapes, draw a short vertical line towards the bottom of the page, connected to another horizontal line that is parallel to the first one you drew. The vertical line signifies a generation gap. In this example our married couple is about to have some kids.

In this example, our lucky couple pictured here has two girls. Bless.

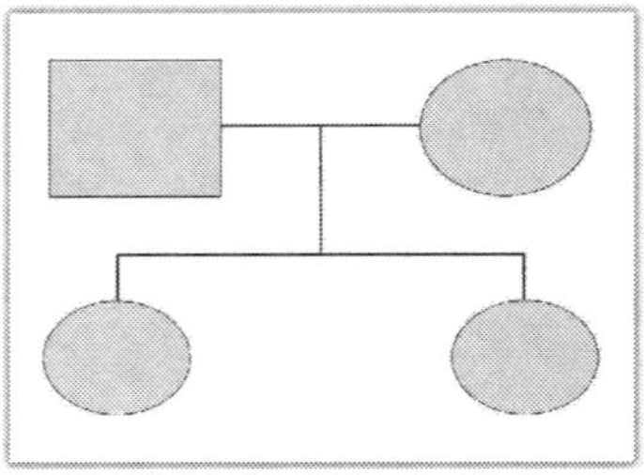

To further flesh out either current or future dependencies that might need to feature in your planning, you can add the couple's parents by drawing a vertical generation gap line extending up towards the top of the page, starting from the middle of each shape of our couple.

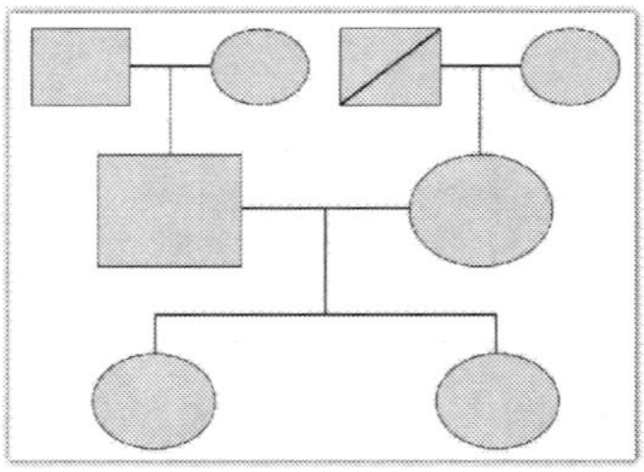

In the example on the right, you can see a diagonal line drawn through the father of the wife of our couple; this represents 'deceased'.

As I said in the last chapter, Family Trees can be fascinating because they tell a multigenerational story of life. Consider the above example expanded to include the siblings of each of the couple, below.

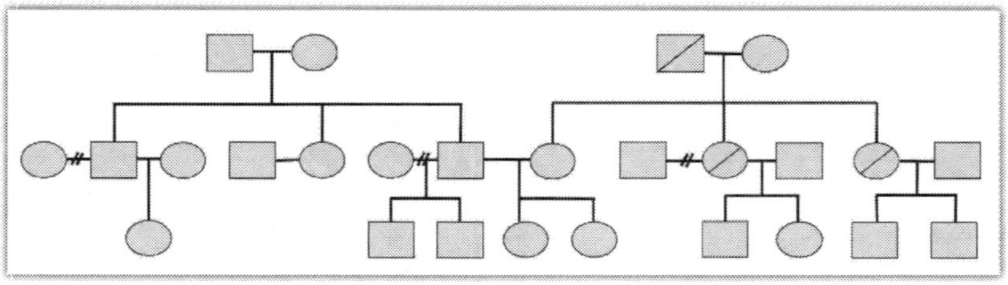

A double line interrupting a horizontal relationship line signifies that the relationship has ended, in this case through divorce. You can see from the picture above that there is quite a story being told across three generations, a story of love and of loss, of death and of renewal with new life.

To complete the above picture, it would be even more helpful to include a name underneath each of the individuals represented, along with that person's age, and even their city/ country of residence.

That's a lot of information available in a single glance. This is a very welcome asset in the hands of a lawyer who is drawing up your last will and testament, but we'll come to that later.

For the time being, now that you've had a quick lesson in drawing up a Family Tree, or at least a family tree that is sufficient for your purposes today, go ahead and draw up your own, complete with names, ages, and residence.

Or am I too late? Have you already started to scribble yours down? Don't you love shortcuts—nothing like an early win to create some momentum . . . ☺.

Adding another dimension

Having already explored the concept of revealing your Must-Haves, and in the shadow of the Family Tree exercise, it's time to merge these two assets into a single, multi-dimensional asset that gives you an even better perspective. This is the Family Timeline asset, one which brings your Must-Haves into the context of the rest of your life as well as the people for whom you're responsible.

You're going to need a fresh piece of paper, or a new file if you're tabletting, and at some point it would be fun to invite your spouse into this exercise, for reasons that should be starting to feel self-evident but that I'll come back to in a minute.

The purpose of the exercise is to take the relevant people from your Family Tree asset and start getting some perspective on the Must-Haves of your future which need to be factored into your planning. By 'relevant people' I mean people who are dependent or codependent on you, at least to some extent. Usually this means spouse and your children, but possibly also relatives who are infirm and live with you or could conceivably be in that position one day (this might be your parents, for example).

Again, the exercise starts with a blank piece of paper or, if you're technologically-minded, a tablet.

About two-thirds from the top of the page draw a horizontal line that spans the page, like an X-axis. Similarly, come in from the left edge of the page a bit and draw a Y-axis, like this picture.

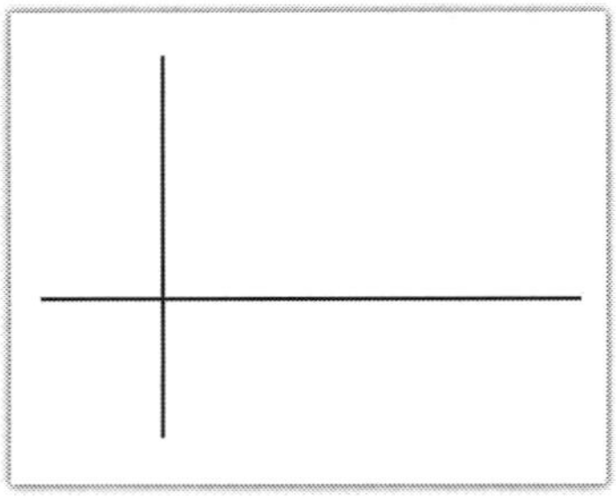

Draw enough lines parallel and below the X-axis so that there are sufficient rows for the individuals you want to include on this chart, using your Family Tree as a guide.

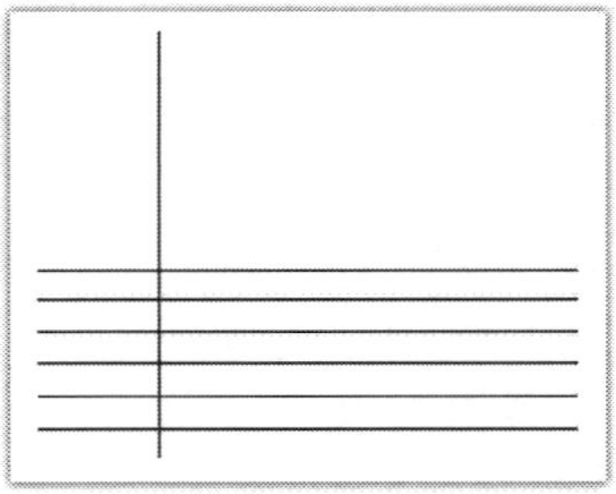

Write the name of those individuals on the inside-left of the Y-axis. In this example here, 'P1' stands for Partner #1, 'C1' stands for 'oldest child', etc. Above the rows write the word 'year'.

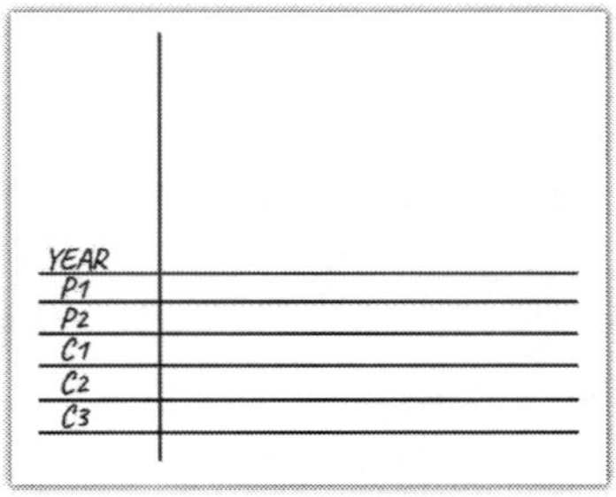

In each row on the left of the Y-Axis, write that individual's age today. At a couple of points as you run your eye across the X-axis, choose a year in the future and update the ages of each individual below that, as you can see in the example pictured here.

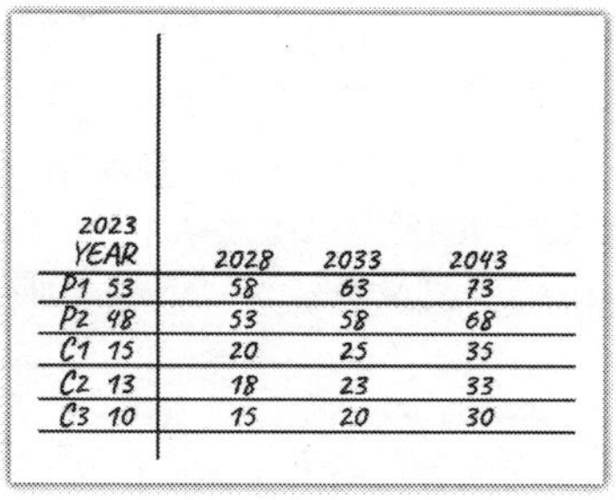

2023 YEAR	2028	2033	2043
P1 53	58	63	73
P2 48	53	58	68
C1 15	20	25	35
C2 13	18	23	33
C3 10	15	20	30

The further into the future you plan out, the better– 1, 3, 5 years, then 10, 15, 20, and 30 years, even. This example has been truncated but you get the idea.

Last step is the fun part—populate events you see happening above the X-axis. This starts with the Must-Haves you've already revealed, but in the context of this Family Timeline, what other events can you see need to be prepared for?

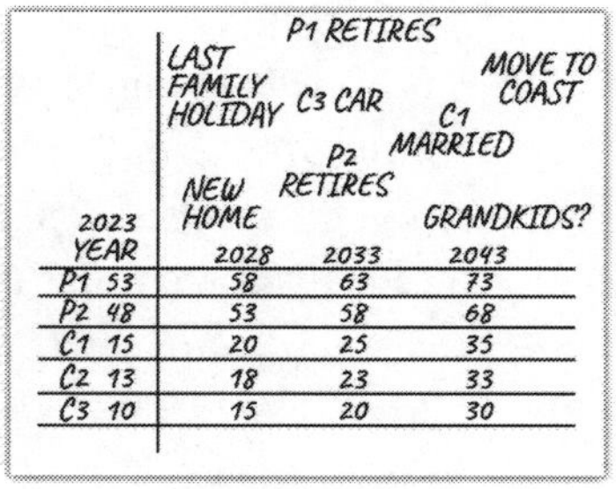

2023 YEAR	2028	2033	2043
P1 53	58	63	73
P2 48	53	58	68
C1 15	20	25	35
C2 13	18	23	33
C3 10	15	20	30

The end result is your must-haves and other significant events located in time with the context of the rest of your life, your age, your family. Here's an example of a completed one.

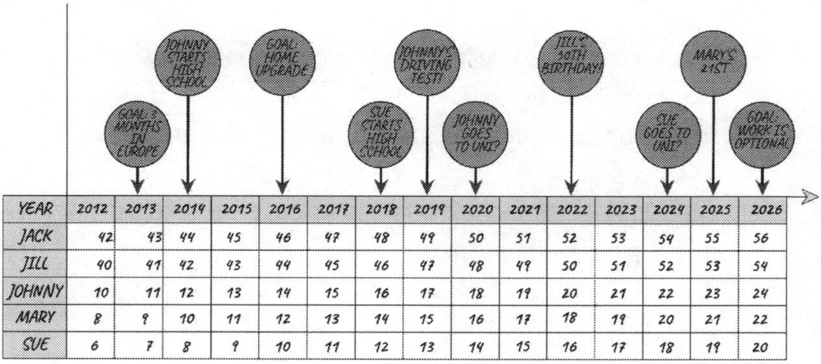

YEAR	2012	2013	2014	2015	2016	2017	2018	2019	2020	2021	2022	2023	2024	2025	2026
JACK	42	43	44	45	46	47	48	49	50	51	52	53	54	55	56
JILL	40	41	42	43	44	45	46	47	48	49	50	51	52	53	54
JOHNNY	10	11	12	13	14	15	16	17	18	19	20	21	22	23	24
MARY	8	9	10	11	12	13	14	15	16	17	18	19	20	21	22
SUE	6	7	8	9	10	11	12	13	14	15	16	17	18	19	20

These two assets provide invaluable context to your team, particularly when they're brainstorming strategies on your behalf or looking at the 'safety' of your must-haves—all subjects we'll come to later in the book.

To get a feel for what can go into this timeline, really lean into this exercise. Spend some time with it and dream a little.

Remember, you don't get a second shot at your time on this planet, so what would you like to see in your future?

Go ahead and draw up your own Family Timeline. To stimulate your thinking, populate your chart by answering the questions below.

About you

- *What hobbies do you wish you'd taken up or qualifications have you always wanted to obtain? Play the piano? Learn Russian? Sculpture? Psychology degree?*
- *By what age do you want to be retired or, at least, expect to phase into retirement? If you're already retired, now that you have the time what would give you joy?*
- *Have you seen the 'Northern Lights' in Norway yet? Or the evening glow of Mt Etna volcano from the viewing deck of a cruise ship off the coast of Sicily? The spring blossoms start to fall in Osaka?*
- *Have you swum with the dolphins in San Diego, watched the whales breaching off the Mexican coast, or gone big game fishing off the west coast of Australia?*

About living

- *How often do you want to replace the family car? Are you a one-car family or two?*
- *Is the family home in need of updating, renovating, extending, or replacing?*
- *Do you need to start thinking about that idea of buying a four-wheel drive and caravan and 'doing a lap' of the country?*
- *Are you thinking it might be nice to sell up and move somewhere warmer?*

About your kids, if you have them.

- *Do you want to help support your kids to buy their first home?*
- *How old do you think your first born will be when he or she marries?*
- *What age does your youngest get a driver's licence?*
- *Do you think your children will have children of their own?*

How old might you be when you start to see grandkids?

- *If your kids are already there, ask this question about your grandchildren.*
- *Have you wanted to take the adult children and their children on an exotic holiday experience to be together as a big fam*ily for a week?

About your parents, if they're still around.

- *By what age do you guess you will have had to put your parents into a nursing home?*
- *How old will your siblings be when it comes time to grasp that nettle?*
- *Do they live in the same city as your parents and can help or will you be flying solo on this chore?*

As for the next most obvious question—where do you keep all these assets? The answer is in your GPS, which we're going to dive right into in just a moment. Before we do, though, there's something missing.

How can I get my spouse involved?

That's a great question, I'm glad I asked it.

The Independent Planning-for-results Method is a process to bulletproof your finances and give you certainty about your financial future. However, it's not just about planning your money, it's about planning your future, too.

In the opening chapters of this book, I said that your finances are an enabler that largely determine your style of life. I also said that this method will work for anyone with an economic engine and a desired future that they would like to bring about on purpose, rather than by luck.

When it comes to planning your finances, often one spouse takes a leading role. However, what I'm really teaching you in this book is how to shape your finances by planning your future. So, if you and your spouse truly intend to live this planned future *together*, it makes sense that you *do* this planning *together*.

Sure, one spouse can take a leading role and push the process along (that'd be you in this case, unless your spouse was the one who handed you this book!), but important decisions seldom happen solo in a relationship like a marriage. Fun ones that endure, anyway.

Important point to make, I think.

Okay, let's march forward towards Bulletproof Future Town using your Roadmap, up next . . .

Ah ha's . . .

- *Planning in a vacuum is not a winning strategy.*
- *The future you're creating needs to factor in where you are today, who you're going to take with you, and what that is likely to look like.*
- *Your Family Tree and Family Timeline are two planning assets that make this simple and easy.*

Chapter 11

Having a Roadmap

"A goal without a plan is just a wish."
—Antoine de Saint-Exupéry

Confronted by disorganised finances and an uncertain future, so far you've seen how the IP4RM can pull order from this chaos soup: your valued direction and meaningful, worthwhile objectives for you and your family.

You're now '*cooking with gas*', as they say in the classics, so you're ready to round out your Roadmap.

In the Independent Planning-for-results Method, your Roadmap *per se*, is actually a toolkit consisting of multiple intellectual property assets you've created to bulletproof your finances so you can confidently realise the future you want for you and your family.

The assets you've created so far are your *Value Chain*, your *Must-Haves*, your *Family Tree* and *Family Timeline*. Before you head off to 'Bulletproof-Finances Town' (right next door to 'Financially Certain Futuresville'), there are a few final items to pack into your toolkit.

A blueprint for your Must-Haves

Your Must-Haves each require some sort of target sum of money by a due date in order to make it happen. Your **Must-Have Blueprint** is an asset that accomplishes two purposes:

1. It contains the key action item to the funding plan stated in clear and concise terms—we call this your 'funding mechanism', and
2. It shows you what 'on track' looks like at regular periods

on the way to the date the Must-Have is accomplished, which we call your 'funding schedule'.

An example: 'Doing a Lap'

Let's say one of your Must-Haves is called "Doing a Lap", a name you've given to your dream of taking the family around the country for 4 months in a huge Winnebago RV. You've done the research and priced the cost of the objective at $100,000. And you want to go before the kids get too old, let's say by Xmas 2030.

Cue the weeds . . .

Is that present value or future value money?

What return are we going to earn here?

Is that gross of investment costs, or net?

What tax rate are we applying to income and gains?

How do we factor in the fact that growth will be larger towards the end of the program than in its initial phases?"

All fair questions but don't let them stop you in your tracks. You want progress, even if there are details yet to be worked out. Here's how you could do that: take out a Must-Have worksheet and write out the details without worrying too much about the financial gymnastics such as the 'funding mechanism' for now.

Must-Have Blueprint		
Name:	Doing a Lap	Feelings on achievement
Due Date:	25 December 2030	Awesome. Connected. A good parent
Target Sum:	$100,000	
Funding mechanism - the key actions required		
(blank)		
Funding schedule - 'on track' lookslike this		
25 Dec 2023	$12,500	
25 Dec 2024	$25,000	
25 Dec 2025	$37,500	
25 Dec 2026	$50,000	
25 Dec 2027	$62,500	
25 Dec 2028	$75,000	
25 Dec 2029	$87,500	
25 Dec 2030	$100,000	

Okay, *now* we can brace ourselves for the questions that would have stopped you previously from following through on a very simple first step. Here's how you solve them without having to become a professor in mathematics.

Go ahead and pull out our old friend, Google, and type in 'savings goal calculator'. Roughly fifty million of them will show up. Pick one. Like this one:

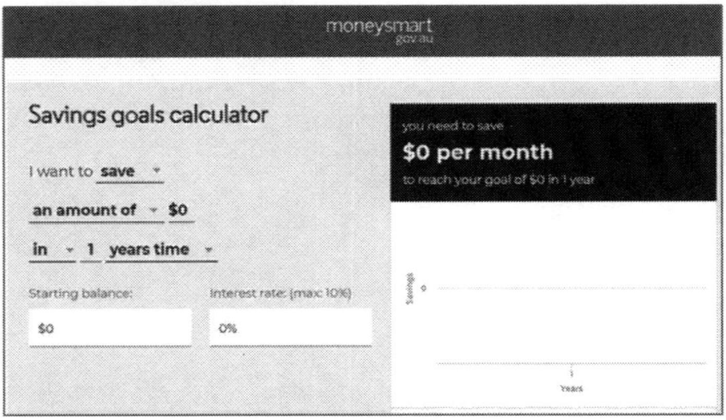

Then fill in the blanks, and it will give you a result, like this:

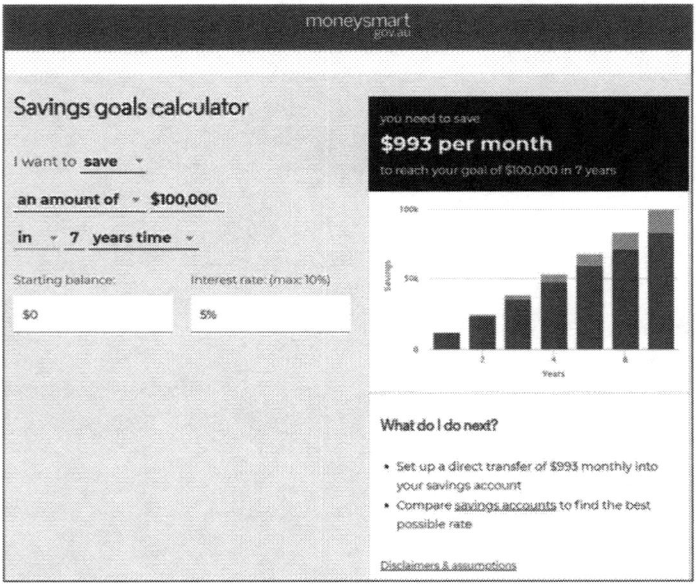

It even gives you some advice, as you can see, about setting up a direct monthly transfer from one bank account to another, plus a link for comparison research on different savings account options.

Turning back to some of the technical questions that you

neatly sidestepped, if you check the disclaimers and assumptions on the website, some of the answers are provided for you.

Present value (PV) dollars versus future value (FV) dollars

In this particular calculator no allowance has been made for inflation eroding the buying power of $100k in 7 years' time. One 'hack' to get around this problem without going on an endless search for the perfect calculator is to assume that the return you're earning is net of inflation. So in the above example you simply conclude that the interest rate you're earning is net of inflation.

Investment costs

Likewise, no allowance is made in this calculator for investment costs or taxation. The same hack works—the 5% interest rate is net of all those costs. What might they be? Perhaps add 1% for investment costs and maybe add a third of the return for taxation.

If you gross up the interest rate used above to account for inflation, fees and tax, you might be aiming at an investment return of 10% gross, say. If your reaction is "*Eek! Where am I going to earn 10% in this day and age?!*" then reduce to an interest rate you're comfortable with. Say that figure waters down the net return to just 2.5%, then what that means is your contribution each month will need to increase. The calculator recalibrates that for us, like the below.

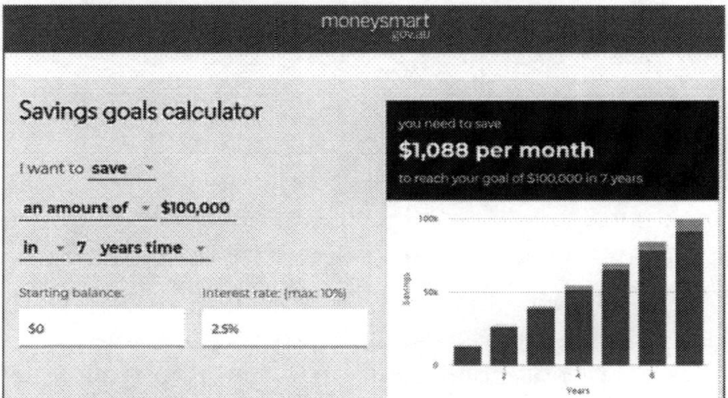

That's the Must-Have Blueprint.

It's a starting point, not an ending point. It's a beacon and signpost, not an actuary's report. It's designed to give you something to aim at and somewhere to start.

More sophisticated objectives like retirement and pension fund calculations might require more sophisticated calculators but remember the purpose of the blueprint at this point in the process. We'll come back to the subject of upscaling your resources later in this book when we get to building your team.

There's one more step to the blueprint and that is to have a written procedure for the funding plan. For example: "*On the first of each month, $1088 is to be transferred from XYZ account into ABC investment program which must earn at least 2.5% per annum after all costs and taxes*." This goes onto the blueprint.

Must-Have Blueprint		
Name:	Doing a Lap	Feelings on achievement
Due Date:	25 December 2030	Awesome. Connected. A good parent
Target Sum:	$100,000	
Funding mechanism - the key actions required		
On the first of each month, $1088 is to be transferred from XYZ account into ABC investment program which must earn at least 2.5% per annum after all costs and taxes.		
Funding schedule - 'on track' lookslike this		
25 Dec 2023	$12,500	
25 Dec 2024	$25,000	
25 Dec 2025	$37,500	
25 Dec 2026	$50,000	
25 Dec 2027	$62,500	
25 Dec 2028	$75,000	
25 Dec 2029	$87,500	
25 Dec 2030	$100,000	

Now you have a tool that is significantly more advanced than a simple wish or goal, yet an asset far more useful than a jargony-report that sits in a bottom drawer collecting dust.

Can you imagine how valuable this blueprint is in the hands of your team so they can really get their heads around what you're trying to accomplish? How much more effective might they be as they brainstorm strategies to get there sooner or identify any risks or potential pitfalls that might obstruct you from achieving your must-haves? Trust me . . . 😉

Financial Snapshots on your journey

One of your last Roadmap assets to take with you on your journey is the **Financial Snapshot**. Its purpose is to give you a simple, 'point-in-time' snapshot of your finances that you feed into the tools you will use to measure your progress (we'll come to these shortly).

The Financial Snapshot is quickly and easily accomplished by using our beloved squares, circles, and lines. You're no longer a novice on these, so here's a concise tutorial on how to create yours . . .

Grab a piece of paper or if you do drawings and scribbles with a tablet, grab that. We start, as always, with you (and your spouse if you're not single), and we do that with a pair of squares, like so:

A square is an asset. A circle is a liability. We draw in the assets and liabilities. We're going to show the flow of cash through the system in a moment. You can see pictured, the family home has been entered attached to a home loan, living expenses and credit card payments, and a share portfolio on the left.

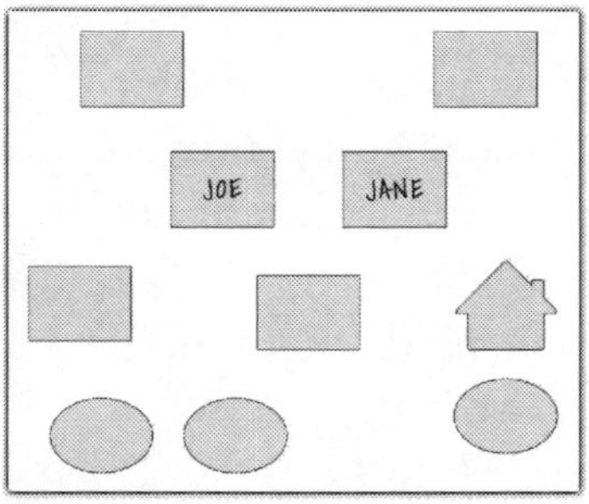

Put in the lines and arrows showing the flow of cash.

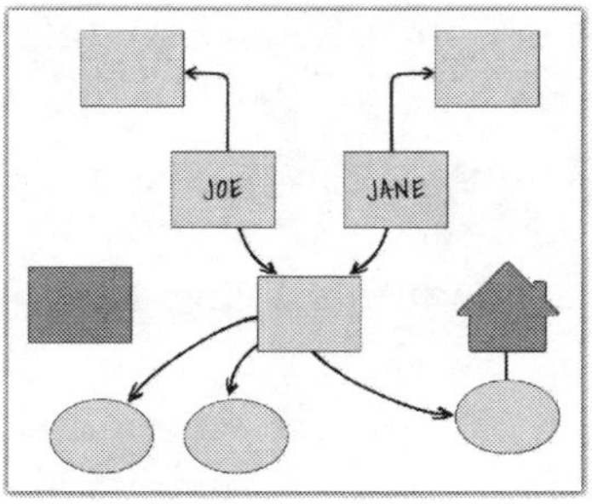

Lastly, the amounts and labels are added so that we can identify what and where is flowing through the system. Note the reference names—the last four digits of the various accounts, for instance, and the names of each of the retirement funds. and add values for each of the cashflows as well as the assets and liabilities. The example we're working on below is complete.

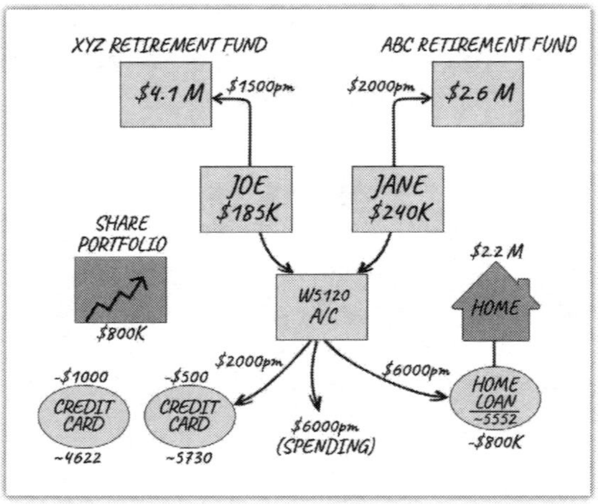

The Financial Shapshot identifies all the significant pieces in your assets, liabilities and cashflows and can grow to be as extensive as you need. Just remember the idea is not to reproduce a high quality balance sheet that would make a registered auditor drool . . . you just want to capture the key items that will feed into your progress reports, which we'll cover off shortly.

Note how the Financial Snapshot not only lets you see everything in one glance, it also shows you how your flow of cash **should** be moving around your Financial House. For instance, in the example above there is a payment of $2000/ month going to each of two credit cards, plus living expenses being accounted for at $6000/month. There is a payment going to the home loan, and payments to Joe and Jane's retirement funds.

Again, the value of this asset is leveraged in the hands of 'Team You', which we'll come to later in the book.

The essential ingredient to staying the course

There is nothing more valuable when it comes to consistent follow-through on a necessary course of action than seeing genuine proof of real progress. In the Independent Planning-for-results Method there are two types of progress you want to see:

1. Progress towards your Must-Haves
2. Progress towards bulletproof finances

These two aspects of progress work together to create a growing sense of confidence about where your finances are headed. Remember, when your finances are 'certified bulletproof' you are making your future secure too, which feeds back into a heightened probability your Must-Haves will be realised as well. This is the reason there are two types of progress reports that work together to fuel your inspiration and encourage you to keep moving forward.

Measuring progress towards your Must-Haves

Quick stock-take: having envisioned a clear and compelling future that you want to bring to life, and to show you're serious about that, you've seen how to create a blueprint for the key must-haves of that future. The next logical extension is to take that blueprint and convert it into a simple chart that you can use to plot your progress, each step of the way.

The medium you can use to do this is basically whatever tickles your fancy, but the idea is to make sure it is simple, visual, and easy to update. Some ideas . . .

A hand-drawn chart that you laminate and put on the wall and update using a coloured flipchart marker.

A portable mini-whiteboard you put somewhere prominent and update with whiteboard markers.

A spreadsheet you create using Microsoft Excel that automatically updates a chart that is based on the spreadsheet and saved to your desktop.

The last one is my go-to, and you'll find a template for you in the resource section towards the end of this book. But for the technically-minded, here's how I do it . . .

First, open up a new spreadsheet and, using the Must-Have Blueprint, copy and paste the funding schedule into it.

Funding schedule - 'on track' looks like this:	
25 Dec 2023	$12,500
25 Dec 2024	$25,000
25 Dec 2025	$37,500
25 Dec 2026	$50,000
25 Dec 2027	$62,500
25 Dec 2028	$75,000
25 Dec 2029	$87,500
25 Dec 2030	$100,000

You will want category labels for the columns to differentiate between your target number and the number you input as you make progress, like the picture below.

	Target	Actual
25-Dec-23	$12,500	
25-Dec-24	$25,000	
25-Dec-25	$37,500	
25-Dec-26	$50,000	
25-Dec-27	$62,500	
25-Dec-28	$75,000	
25-Dec-29	$87,500	
25-Dec-30	$100,000	

Rearrange the dates onto an X-axis and the target sums onto the Y-axis. This isn't a tutorial on the features of Excel; the program does the hard work for you automatically if you give it the parameters, like the picture below.

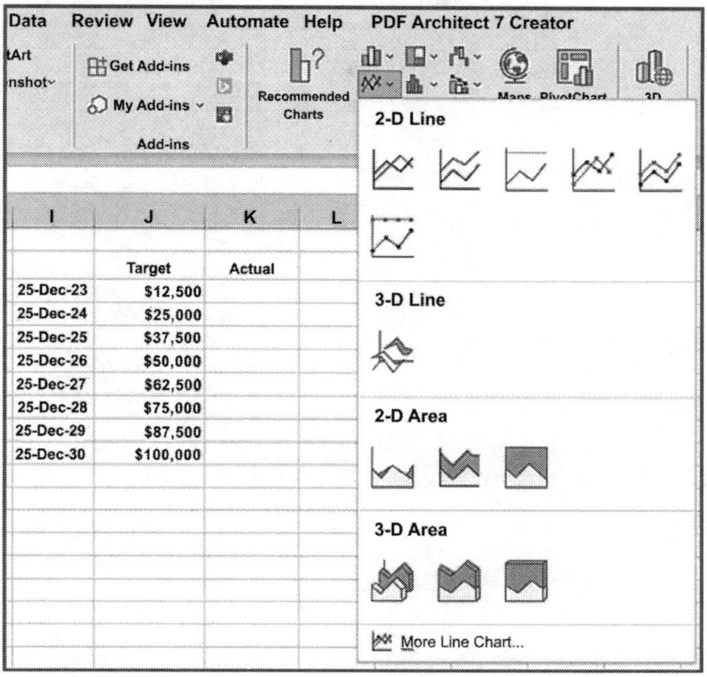

Once you've selected the graph you want it will look something like the image below.

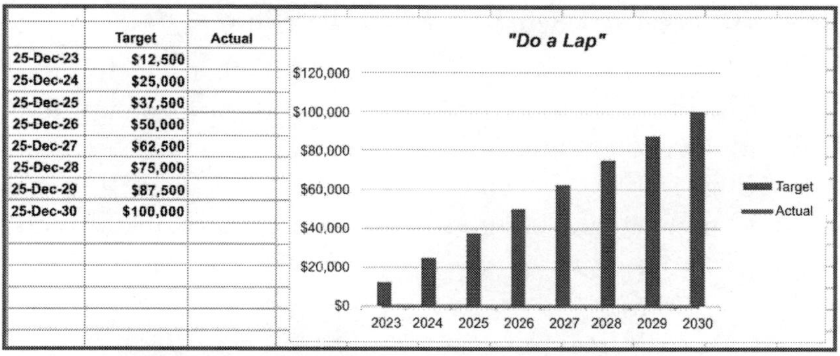

As you monitor your progress, you populate the Actuals column, and this updates on the chart which you can format to your heart's content and leave on your desktop or print out and stick somewhere you can see it easily during your day.

	Target	Actual
25-Dec-23	$12,500	$3,500
25-Dec-24	$25,000	$18,500
25-Dec-25	$37,500	$31,000
25-Dec-26	$50,000	$68,500
25-Dec-27	$62,500	$56,000
25-Dec-28	$75,000	$60,000
25-Dec-29	$87,500	$85,000
25-Dec-30	$100,000	$99,500

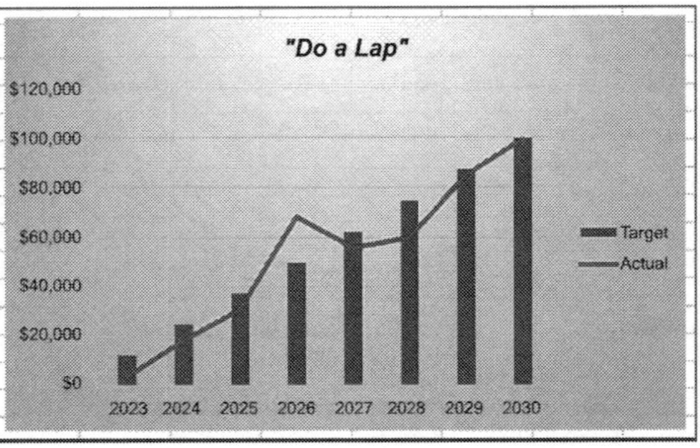

Not rocket science, I'm sure you'll agree, and for good reason: we don't want to let 'perfect get in the way of good enough'. The Pareto Principle is alive and well when it comes to all these assets and so, if you're like me and tend towards perfectionism, then you need to remain vigilant here, or else you'll burn a bunch of time coming up with something which, ironically, impedes your progress instead of supporting it.

Create one of these assets for each of your Must-Haves and update them at each of your progress meetings, an event we'll explore next chapter.

Optimising your finances so they're bulletproof

Cast your mind way back to Chapter 4 when I introduced the core principle behind the Independent Planning-for-results Method's whole philosophy: getting your financial house in order. This feat is achieved by looking at the individual rooms of your Financial House and tidying each of them up. To whit, you have a room for . . .

1. Your cash
2. Your wealth
3. Your tax
4. Your legals
5. Your risks

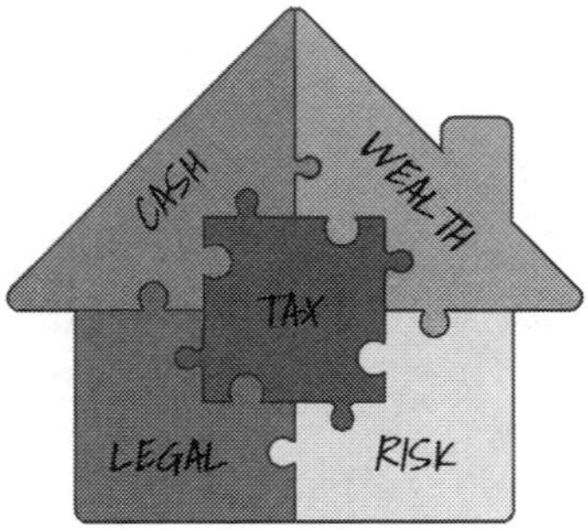

What's getting organised even mean?

Coming up with a metric that shows you how organised you are isn't as complicated as it first might appear. We've already experienced this as children, in fact.

To get your head around this concept, think back to the report card we used to get as kids at school. Your report card was an indicator of the state of your 'scholastic house' which, although not 100% predictive of a successful life after school, definitely contributes to making success more likely.

Your report card helped your parents understand how well you were doing academically because it broke your scholastic house down into its individual parts: maths, science, phys-ed, English, history, etc., etc. That made it possible to establish how much more work there was to do in that particular area to get you in great shape and well prepared for life after school. If you were a straight-A student, then your parents could rest easy, your scholastic house was in good order.

As far as your financial house is concerned, being a straight-A student means your finances are bulletproof. This, in turn, means that you are entitled to feel very confident about your future coming to fruition as you've intended.

What does success look like?

By breaking your financial house down into its five rooms, you're not only massively simplifying your finances, you're also making it possible to determine where you stand in terms of how well organised you are, financially. I'll show you what I mean ...

Let's appraise your current organisational status in the area of the 'Cash Planning' room of your financial house. To do that we return to Chapter 4 where we established the building blocks of cash planning. It incorporated:

your personal cashflows (the ins and outs of your money each month),

- your banking arrangements (where that cash gets allocated and how you access it when you need it),

- credit and finance (which you use to acquire assets that grow or depreciate in value),
- the operation of your investments and retirement accounts, and
- your entitlements to social security.

What would be an ideal outcome in each of these elemental building blocks? Here are some suggestions . . .

Cash Planning	What success looks like
In the last twelve months I've completely reviewed **my personal cashflows** and can confirm that . . .	. . . I'm living within my means and amply funding all my Must-Haves according to the funding plan in their blueprints. I have an allocation plan aligned with my objectives for all income I receive over the next twelve months and all expenses I incur over that time.
In the last twelve months I've completely reviewed **my banking arrangements** and can confirm that . . .	. . . my accounts are low-fee, simple, accessible, reconciled monthly and dove-tail into my tax returns.
In the last twelve months I've completely reviewed **my credit and finance arrangements** and can confirm that . . .	. . . I carry only necessary and manageable consumer debt, all my liabilities are set on the lowest interest rates sensibly possible, and my payments are forecast to extinguish the debt on a timescale that makes sense to my overall Roadmap.

In the last twelve months I've completely reviewed **my investments and retirement accounts/pension funds** and can confirm that . . .	. . . all my portfolios are properly diversified, being managed according to an independently verifiable strategy that only take risks that bear worthwhile rewards. The cost of operation is very reasonable compared to similar portfolios and accounts. The performance is top quartile compared with a suitable benchmark with a comparable risk/reward profile.
In the last twelve months I've completely reviewed **my social security entitlements** and can confirm that . . .	. . . I am receiving all my entitlements and have considered and decided against alternative restructures to my arrangements that might achieve additional benefits.

Sound like 'optimised cash planning' to you? It should, it is!

Equipped with this insight, you now have incredible appraisal power in your hands. You've established one book-end on a whole spectrum of 'cash planning orderliness' . . . which means the opposite of the above would be the other book-end, a state of complete disorder in your cash planning. Also, you're able to use this to conceive of what features typify various points in between cash planning order and disorder.

Developing your own 'Bulletproof Progress Report Card'

You're ready to put this into practice so you can measure your progress towards bulletproof.

Step 1.

Using the above breakdown as a guide, go back to each of the remaining four rooms of your financial house—wealth, tax, risk and legal—and similarly identify what success looks like to you in each of those areas. This will give you your 'what success looks like' end of the metric.

Step 2.

To flesh out the 'extreme disorder' end of the metric, make some notes about what constitutes failure.

Step 3.

Make some notes about what milestones would be visible at various points in between both extremes. For instance, what would constitute a five-out-of-ten? You can use a graphic like the one below.

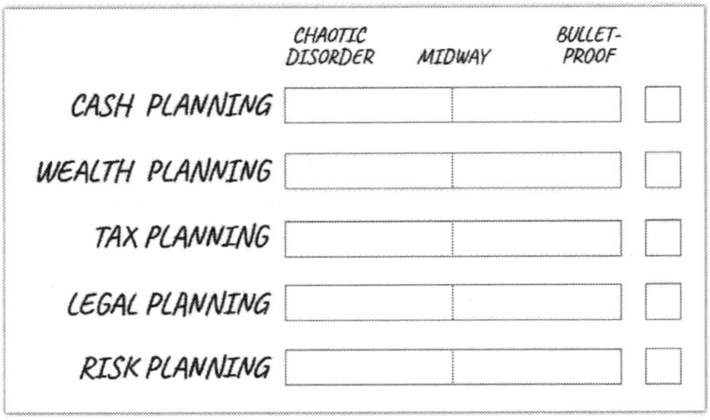

Step 4.

Rate yourself as of today. You can't fudge this, you'd only be fooling yourself. Give it some thought, consider each of the elements of each metric and rate yourself. Here's an example of what your report card might look once completed with your own appraisal of your own metrics.

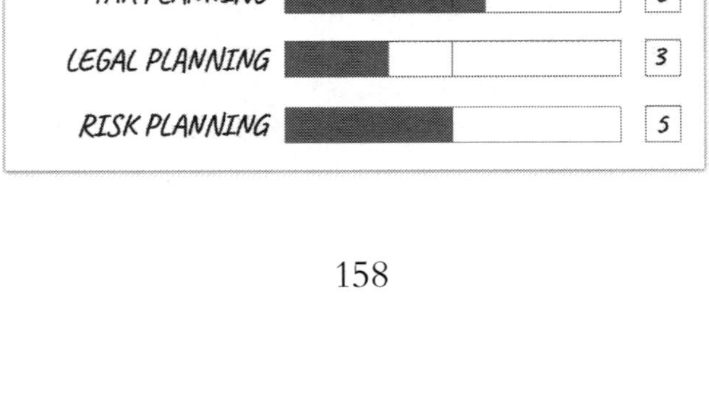

Okay. Well done.

You've now got an asset that you update in each progress meeting that shows you in one glance how you're progressing towards your objective of bulletproof finances. Like all the assets you're developing as part of your Roadmap, the value is giving you that little bit of motivation you need to keep your momentum moving you forward towards the destination.

Deep breath. It's time to tie all this together . . .

Ah ha's . . .

- *Your Roadmap is not some weighty tome that sits in the bottom drawer collecting dust but a toolkit of simple-but-highly valuable tools you use to pull order out of chaos.*
- *These elements of your Roadmap are living, breathing assets that evolve as your finances develop. You pack these tools into your toolkit to take on your journey to your bulletproof financial future.*

Chapter 12

Tying It All Together

"Your life will be no better than the plans you make and the action you take. You are the architect and the builder of your own life, fortune and destiny."

—Alfred A. Montapert

In this chapter, we're going to pull together all the work you've done to date into an event I call the **Progress Meeting.** Lots of things happen in those meetings, but they're not called *progress* for nothing. In your journey to a bulletproof future, the progress meeting is a celebratory event that exists for two purposes:

- Firstly, to mark the progress you're making on your quest, and
- To confirm what needs to be done before the next scheduled progress meeting so you keep making transparent and clear progress.

"*A meeting with myself?*" I hear you exclaim. *"That's cuckoo!"*

What, you've never put an appointment into your calendar to guarantee some uninterrupted 'me time' and get something important done? Sure you have.

Look—to describe these meetings as important is an understatement, which is why we don't leave them to chance.

No more ado. Let's get this done.

Populating your GPS

In Chapter Six I introduced you to 'the backbone' of the

IP4R Method, an asset called the 'Global Positioning System', or GPS for short.

Your GPS is an incredibly powerful tool for two reasons: firstly because it's the link between your planning and the results that come from following your plan, but it also does most of the heavy lifting in terms of getting your Financial House in order—and keeping it organised for good.

Having now built out your toolkit with high quality assets that will serve the dual purpose of Roadmap and Cheerleading Squad, it's time to populate your GPS so nothing is left out and everything is where it should be when you need it.

This exercise is a little involved but, in fairness, we are 'tying all this together'. So if you don't have the time or presence of mind to follow through on the exercise now, that's fine, bookmark this and come back to it later, just follow along for now.

(In fact, if you are starting to feel this way about lots of these elements, then let me reassure you: it's okay to ask for help. There are numerous step-off points sprinkled through this book for you to do just that, if you're feeling like you want to call in the cavalry.)

Anyway, back to the action: take out a fresh sheet of paper or, if you are creating these assets electronically, then a new file on your device. The format of the asset itself is a matter of personal preference. I find that Microsoft Word or Excel is just fine but anything that can create a table is what you want. Whatever style takes your fancy here are four key features it needs to have:

1. A 'headline row' where you can write in the date of each scheduled progress meeting,
2. Several rows within each progress meeting to enter in tasks that need to be done,
3. A way to note down who is responsible for each particular task (their initials is fine), and
4. Space where you will indicate whether the task is complete, abandoned or outstanding (a smiley face icon works well for complete, an X for abandoned, and a blank for outstanding).

Your first entry is going to be the progress meeting you're holding right now, today ☺. So in the headline row, enter "Due by Progress Meeting" and today's date. If you've followed the advice of this book so far, you'll already have created several assets, so you can enter them into this GPS and tick them off as having been done. If you've followed the instructions above, you should have something that is roughly equivalent to the table below:

Due by progress meeting 20/6/23		
Create Values Chain	AB	☺
Complete Must-Haves Exercise	AB	☺
Create Family Tree	AB	☺
Create Family Timeline	AB	☺
Create GPS	AB	☺

Nice. Now follow these steps.

1. Insert a number of additional lines so that you have plenty of space for additional progress meetings and their task rows.
2. Next, scroll down to the next progress meeting. What's the date in 30 days' time? Write that date into the meeting name. Scroll down to the next progress meeting and write the date for 60 days' time and again for 90 days' time. Your progress meetings are going to be spaced out further apart than this in future, but that's how it's going to work at the start.

Due by progress meeting 20/6/23		
Create Values Chain	AB	☺
Complete Must-Haves Exercise	AB	☺
Create Family Tree	AB	☺
Create Family Timeline	AB	☺
Create GPS	AB	☺
Due by progress meeting 31/7/23		
Due by progress meeting 31/8/23		

Very nice.

3. Now go to the next blank progress meeting name and where you'd normally write the date, write a year only, put in next year, e.g. if this year is 2023, then write '2024'. From that point, skip three progress meetings forward, leaving them blank, and at the next occurring progress meeting write the following year (continuing this example, '2025'). Continue this until you have got ten years' worth of progress meetings populated.

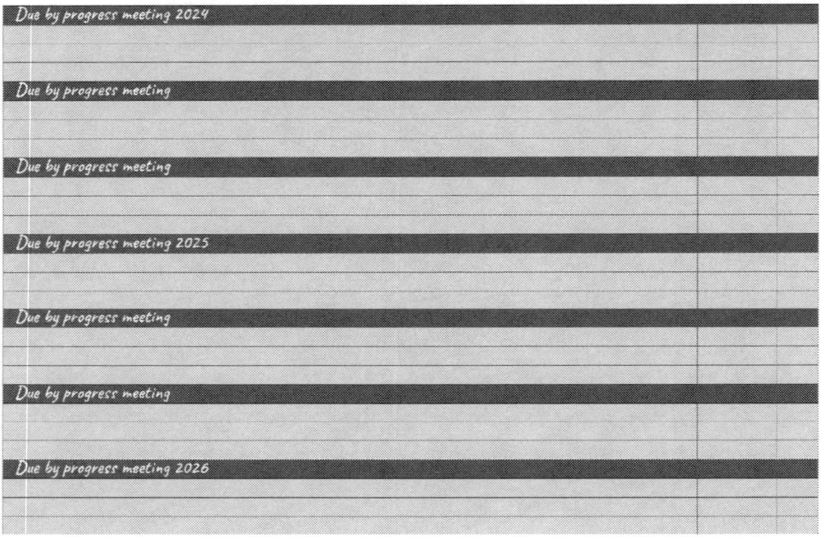

Excellent. As simple as this task was, as small a step as it was, it's a giant leap in bulletproofing your finances and creating more certainty in your financial future. Keep walking forward . . .

4. Open your Family Tree asset you created earlier in this book. Put each individual's next birthday into your GPS. To do that, find the closest progress meeting in your GPS that occurs BEFORE their next birthday and write the equivalent of: "James turns 20 on 25/9/23."
5. Pull out your Family Timeline asset from earlier in this book. If you've genuinely put your best effort into that simple exercise, you'll have some gold nuggets there, which you're going to carry over into your GPS. If the event occurs after the last progress meeting slot that you

have available in your table so far, then in that otherwise empty last slot, enter the event from your Family Timeline, preceded by "extend GPS and insert:" in front of the event. For example, if the Family Timeline event is "buy a beach house by 25/12/2040" then go to the last available progress meeting and write "extend GPS and insert: buy a beach house by 25/12/2040." Do that now.

Nice job. Now remember the conversation you and I had last chapter about your other half, your spouse? You both need to be on the same page if this is going to work, so . . .

6. . . . add this to your GPS, if you haven't already: "Have a conversation with spouse to show him/her this book I'm reading."

The same is true of anyone else whose expertise or cooperation you're going to need to help you get things done. For instance, later in this book we'll talk a little about how you can go about enlisting some help by selecting 'subject matter experts' to be a part of your team. To get them on the same page as you, they really need to know where you're coming from and what it is you're trying to accomplish. That way you minimise the chances of mixed messages or outright conflicting agendas.

So add a note to this effect as a reminder for later, when you have digested the content yet to come about building your team:

7. "*Ask SMEs if they're prepared to read the book.*" (And if so, ask them to tell you when they have finished it and confirm whether they're prepared to be involved in this project of yours called bulletproofing your finances for a certain future.)

Brilliant. Now insert your financial objectives and milestones, like this:

8. Go through your Must-Have worksheets and carry them across into the dates when they need to be achieved by. The entry could read something like this: "Must-Have: 'Do a Lap' happens on 25 December 2030."
9. Open up your Must-Have Blueprints and carry across each of the funding schedule dates into the

corresponding dates in your GPS. For instance, in the 'Do a Lap' example, there is a funding milestone on 25 December 2023; so in the progress meeting that occurs before that date you'd enter the following entry: "Must-Have 'Do a Lap' funding mechanism needs to be valued at $12,500 to be 'on track' by 25/12/2023."

Recall that one of the useful functions of your GPS is also to take worries and anxieties out of your head and have them safely tucked away somewhere else for dealing with later. This frees you from having to waste unnecessary emotional energy catastrophising or ruminating on riddles at 3am.

Remember the brain dump exercise you did in Chapter 6? This was an exercise in decluttering your mind by downloading all those gnawing worries and anxieties out of your head and onto a piece of paper where they can be unpacked later, when you've got the time and resources to solve them. This included all the incomplete tasks, 'to do' reminders, projects you've been meaning to start—the whole lot. Here's payday for that particular investment you made . . .

10. Divide that brain dump into 'things that matter' and 'clutter list'. Put a date on the things that matter and enter them into your GPS as a reminder to schedule time to think about them (not at 3am). The stuff that's left, the clutter, doesn't belong in your GPS because by definition, it's unimportant. But it's still unresolved so add to your next scheduled progress meeting "chip away at the clutter list", and put the list to the side, safe in the knowledge that it will be dealt with at the appropriate time.

Your bulletproofing has begun, and your future is already more certain. You're now ready to fill in the rest of that picture so you can start getting tangible results.

Checking in . . .

Take a moment to review your GPS, and reflect on what you've actually done so far today because the reality is you've done something that most people simply don't do. You've taken a leading hand in preparing proactively for future events. Even this simple step increases the likelihood you'll be better prepared for the future. We call it 'living life on purpose'.

In the next revision of your GPS you're going to insert tasks that help you prepare for events that are NOT likely but—if they do occur—you'll be ready.

Does this look like being organised to you? Can you see how having your Financial House in this sort of shape means you have a *significantly higher probability* of making the future you want come to life, by design? Your bullet-proofing is well advanced, and that means your future is already more certain.

There's something else at play here, too . . .

None of what we've covered so far relies on earning great returns from the investment markets, nor that the economy is buoyant, nor world events being predictable and stable. Instead, you're taking clear, confident steps entirely within your control to improve your circumstances and your outlook.

This is what we mean when we say that the Independent Planning for Results Method puts *you* back in the driver's seat, creating the future *you* want to experience. As you continue to put in the work to optimise and bulletproof your finances, the more real that experience becomes . . . until that happy day when it arrives and you get to meet the future you've designed in person . . . ☺

Holding successful progress meetings

You already spend several hours a year planning Christmas and the next family holidays, why not invest another 45 minutes planning the rest of your future? That's right, 45 minutes. That's all a progress meeting takes, tops.

At the outset of this chapter I explained how progress meetings exist to mark your progress (in more ways than one) as well as to keep up your momentum in bulletproofing your future. You've heard me say before that just thinking about exercise doesn't get you physically fit, it's the (consistent) doing that brings results. Well, if accountability is your personal kryptonite, then progress meetings are your salvation.

Making your Must-Haves a reality doesn't happen by chance—work must be done to bear fruit. The ability of this entire framework to deliver you the incredible results that are available for you hinges on your accountability to get the tasks done that bulletproofing requires.

The point is this: the work needs to be done so these meetings *need to happen*. To that extent they're a critical ingredient in the Independent Planning-for-results Method, and so we don't leave them to chance. They need to be held at regular intervals and run according to a set agenda.

Let's dive a little deeper into what progress meetings need to look like to get the most from them.

The Quarterly Sprint

They say that life is a marathon, full of milestones. A sprint, though, happens over shorter distances with one milestone in mind: the finish line. The IP4R Method is deployed in a series of sprints which enable significant milestones to be achieved one after another. Before you know it, you've run a marathon.

A year is too long to sprint, but if you divide a year up into four quarters, that's a sprint of just 90 days. That's long enough to get some real results and short enough to concentrate on just a few key things. Although in the first year of your experience with this Method you're going to have more progress meetings than that, you'll move into a quarterly schedule thereafter, at least until you first achieve your status of bulletproof (more on what that's like later, by the way!).

Your progress meetings are already in your GPS but if you haven't scheduled them into your personal calendar, go ahead and do that now.

Leaving nothing to chance

This isn't called the 'Take a Wild Guess and See What Happens Method'. It's the *Planning-for-results* Method. It's all about delivering *predictable* and *reliable* results, like clockwork

—*provided you follow the Method.* This is accomplished with forethought and preparation. You can rest assured that unnecessary items have already been weeded out of the Method, and any legitimate deficiencies have already been included. What you see, works.

The purpose of your progress meetings is to obtain an overwhelming sense of confidence that everything that can be done to bulletproof your future is well and truly underway. That's why your progress meetings stick to an agenda.

Here's what you need to make sure you include in yours . . .

1. Planning and Progress (< 20 mins)
    a. Game face ON (2 mins)
    b. Eyes on the prize (5 mins)
    c. Progress: accomplishing the Must-Haves (5 mins)
    d. Progress: optimising to a bulletproof future (3 mins)
    e. Review GPS (5 mins)
2. Deep thinking (< 20 mins)
    a. Strategy brainstorming
       or
    b. Expecting the unexpected
3. Decluttering (5 mins)

These three sections ensure that all the important, planned tasks are resolved, nothing is missed, and that anything that has arisen 'on the fly' since the last meeting, as noted down in the GPS, is likewise dealt with according to its importance and urgency.

Unpacking each agenda item

Progress meetings are intended to be enjoyable—they're a celebration of progress, after all, so they're a positive experience, for sure. But there's a serious side to them, too. They exist to deliver you an important outcome, which is the reason there's no room for confusion and no fat in the agendas.

They're also not a place to do the work that should have been done in preparation for this meeting. They're more to look at the results of that work and plan what needs to be done to prepare for the next meeting. Stay vigilant on this score, otherwise your meetings will (a) drag on, and (b) not be fun.

Make them fun; they're intended and designed to be a champagne moment.

Game face ON

First item on the agenda is to get your game face on. You do that by spending a minute or two reviewing each of your Value Chains so you can reconnect with your reasons for holding this meeting in the first place.

Remember that, to stay on your valued direction, your Value Chain is your framework for making good decisions out of all the options that are constantly calling to you. So pull out each of your Value Chains and walk each other up the links as we did in Chapter 8.

Eyes on the prize

Pull out your Must-Haves and walk through what you want to accomplish, by when, and revisit your thoughts and feelings about that, like we did in Chapter 9.

Are they still Must-Haves? If your juices aren't flowing then is it possible they've dimmed into 'optionals'? Do they still deserve your (and your team's) full commitment?

Does any need to be amended to get them back into priority #1? Does the name need to change, the money required, the due date? Is anything missing?

Also spend a moment asking whether there are any new Must-Haves that are creeping into your world which need to be added into your Roadmap. If so, repeat the exercise from Chapter 9.

Progress: accomplishing the Must-Haves

If the progress meeting is supposed to be an enjoyable experience, then this is the birthplace of joy. A major intended take-away from the progress meeting is an overwhelming sense of confidence you're on track to your desired future, and your Progress Charts are a big part of that. The job is:

1. to compare this meeting's charts against last meeting's charts to see what sort of progress has been made, and
2. to ask whether you're still on track. If you are on track, keep up the good work; if not, what needs to be done to get back on track?

The GPS will shoulder a lot of the load for the second question, but if anything occurs to you, make a note to include it in the GPS.

You might be wondering when you address the questions of investment performance metrics and investment risk ratios. The answer is not here. These are important issues but they're not relevant to what's within your control, such as how much you should contribute to achieve the goal, if the current performance trend continues.

The question of whether your portfolio has the right risk allocations and if its peer-performance appropriate . . . these are actually questions about how well organised this room of your financial house is, which is next on the agenda.

Progress: optimising to a bulletproof future

This part of the meeting is also a joyful experience because it is the tangible evidence of your financial progress towards bulletproofing, which in turn will enhance your Must-Have progress charts in due course. The job is:

1. To compare this meeting's charts against last meeting's charts to see what sort of progress has been made, and
2. To ask whether you're still on track. If you are on track, keep up the good work; if not, what needs to be done to get back on track?

Again, your GPS will shoulder a lot of the load for the second question, but if anything occurs to you, make a note to include it in the GPS, next on the agenda.

Review GPS

I say again: this meeting is not intended to be a replacement for doing the work that was supposed to be done in preparation for today's meeting. If ever you're going to slip into that particular quagmire, then this part of the meeting is when it's most likely. Stay vigilant and call it out if you see it happening.

This document has already been populated and so it takes over as the agenda, really, and you just 'follow the bouncing ball'.

It will include status updates on particular tasks or projects, reports from members of your team, and making notes about what needs to be added to future meetings for follow up. If there are any incomplete tasks that need rescheduling then this is the time to roll them over and identify who is responsible for getting it done.

If there are any incomplete items that keep showing up, ask whether this task is still relevant and necessary, and review its 'must be done by' date. It might be time to Identify and call in a well-placed third party who can help to address this recurrent incomplete.

Review upcoming significant milestones and blocks of work and confirm what needs to be completed before the next scheduled progress meeting and by whom. Ensure you obtain the responsible party's commitment to get their task done by the due date, that they have all the resources necessary to deliver, and that their deliverable is clear so there's no confusion about what success looks like and no possibility of coming to that meeting with a partially incomplete task.

Preparing for the next progress meeting—updating the GPS several weeks ahead of the next scheduled progress meeting includes checking in with third parties to ensure they're on track with their work, reminding them you're expecting their deliverable by the due date and confirming that they're clear on what success looks like.

Strategy brainstorming OR expecting the unexpected

This is a focussed exercise that is either about brainstorming better ways to achieve your Must-Haves ('Strategy Brainstorming': a review of your Plan A), or troubleshooting potential obstacles and risks to your Must-Haves ('Expecting the Unexpected': a review of your Plan B).

You alternate between the two in subsequent meetings—so the first progress meeting you hold you'll run a Strategy Brainstorm, the next progress meeting you'll run an Expect the Unexpected, and the next progress meeting back to Strategy Brainstorm, and so on.

Strategy brainstorming

Is there a better way?

Presently you're executing a specific set of strategies in each of the areas of your Financial House, your Plan A. Some aspects of your Plan A might have a shelf life. This can occur because of external events—e.g. the markets move, the economy changes, world events transpire—or from events closer to home—you get a promotion or take a career change, a new dependent appears on the horizon, something happens to someone you know or you hear about some event in the media and it prompts you to revisit how you're addressing this particular issue in your life.

Ask yourself whether there might be a better way to accomplish what you're doing. The more knowledge and talent you invite into these conversations, the better the results. This means including the considered opinions of independent third parties who possess expertise in the particular areas you're examining.

For example, if you're brainstorming ways to create wealth, an investment expert; if you're brainstorming insurance coverage, an insurance expert; if you're brainstorming tax strategies, a tax expert. You get the idea.

Expecting the unexpected

What obstacles might impact our Must-Haves?

At its heart, this exercise is risk management. I love risk management. Don't judge me.

The central purpose of this exercise is to brainstorm all the possible obstacles that might delay or derail your objectives and analyse what to do about them.

You do this first by identifying each possible obstacle

—whether it's an external event or an internal event—and looking at the likelihood and consequence of each.

Next you ask whether something needs to be done about each. What are your options? What are the pros and cons of each? Which is the best course of action?

Who is going to be responsible for the delivery? Who is going to be tasked with executing the work required?

These are repeatable exercises, which means each time you run them you develop your skill, which means your results will improve in line with your proficiency.

Decluttering

The last item on the agenda deals with all the 'stuff' from the phrase "Stuff Happens", like we talked about back in Chapter 6. Here's the thing . . .

If you leave stuff lying around, it clutters up your head. Clutter generally shows up in the form of emotionally provocative external events beyond your control that seem relevant at two in the morning. This relevancy carries an emotional charge that robs you of a good night's sleep.

Clutter is the polar opposite of organised and will, if left unaddressed, railroad your progress. To avoid being railroaded, jot this clutter down into your GPS: no longer cluttering your head, no longer obstructing your clear thinking or your sleep.

This part of your progress meeting is where you pull up all that clutter and examine it, in the cold, hard light of day, to make doubly sure that it is indeed clutter and can be thrown away, never to return. If there are any diamonds in that rough that ought not to be thrown out, then you can prioritise it.

You accomplish this by looking at each particular item and asking "Is it important?" and, if so, "Is it urgent?." The appropriate way to deal with it is revealed in your answers. This exercise ensures that your progress is not unnecessarily slowed by clutter, but also nothing important is missed inadvertently. Again, this is another learnable skill which gets better with practice.

Progress Meetings: 3 Dos and 3 Don'ts

One of my many personality flaws is an unconcealable intolerance for badly run meetings.

If that particular gripe speaks to you too, then come to my arms, my friend. The proliferation of online meetings during the COVID-19 pandemic was particularly difficult for you and me, wasn't it? An endless stream of pointless meetings we didn't need to be at, hosted and run by someone whose hidden agenda was wanting to be liked by everyone or—even worse—run by someone who was on some sort of power head trip.

The hideous chit-chat. The pointless stories. The self-involved impulses to share every random thought or ill-considered opinion (opinions are like nipples—everyone's got them but that doesn't mean we want to see yours). Or the greatest sin: doing the work live, in front of everyone, that should have been brought to the meeting finished. Oh man.

Perhaps you're a meeting veteran. Perhaps it's not your thing. Pay attention to these Dos and Don'ts and you'll boost your chances of success significantly.

Do enjoy them.

Connect with each other. You're creating the future you envisioned and you're doing it on purpose. What a great team you are. More power to you.

Do appreciate their significance.

Effective meetings will deliver you a successful experience overall. That will have knock-on benefits for your own personal mental and physical health. Your marriage will benefit from this, too. So will your children and your family as a whole.

Do lead them.

Whether you are flying these meetings solo or whether you have invited guests or regular team members present, this is your future. Delegate the tasks, but the responsibility for an effective meeting is yours. Have fun, yes, but go into them with your game face on.

Don't let them drag on.

The longer the meeting, the less effective it becomes. Don't let the meeting go on for so long that it loses its purpose or its energy.

Don't wander off agenda.

Don't allow the meeting to get too distracted by tangents, interesting stories and anecdotes, or off-agenda items being introduced at the last minute. If the subject at hand isn't directly related to the big picture outcome, then it needs to be shut down.

Don't walk away empty-handed.

This is 'Management 101': the meeting shouldn't end without clear agreement as to homework items that will be done 'offline', outside of the meeting environment, and by whom. Always make sure you make it clear what success looks like, what is expected to be delivered by the due date, confirm what resources this individual might need to do their job, and, most importantly, obtain their commitment to deliver.

Follow these tips and your progress meetings will be fun and satisfying. You'll walk away from each of them with a renewed sense of vigour and confidence, and an abiding feeling of peace, that you're walking the path you choose.

Building skill in the various elements of your progress meetings transforms a feeling of confidence to one of inevitability.

Your Optimise-to-Bulletproof Checklist

As time trundles along, you continue holding your progress meetings, executing your Plan A and Plan B reviews, and making progress towards your Must-Haves and becoming bulletproof. Unless you're a goldfish, you'll start to notice something: certain tasks seem to come up again and again.

Cue your **Bulletproof Checklist**.

There are assets and there are *assets*. And although the value of the Plan A and Plan B exercises can potentially be utterly priceless, this one is 'next level'.

If you work out consistently, you'll start to enjoy all the benefits of being fit. If you stop working out, however, and do nothing to keep yourself in shape, your fitness begins to fade. So too your financial fitness—once you've got your Financial House 100% in order, the tasks on your Bulletproof Checklist are what **keeps** it there.

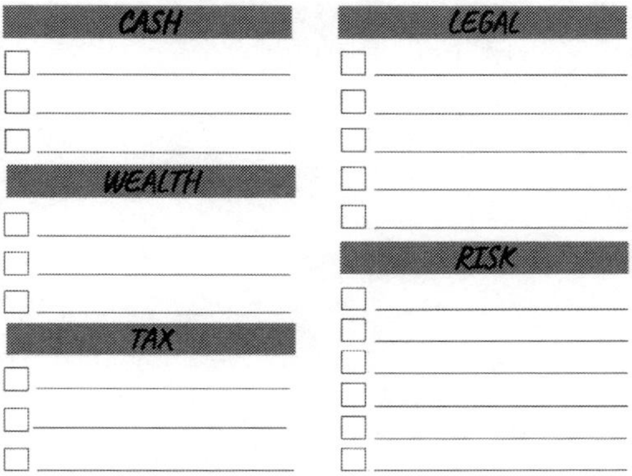

Your Bulletproof Checklist is so very valuable because you will build it simply by going through your journey to becoming financially organised. All you need to do is capture the recurrent tasks into an organised list. There's nothing extra really you have to do, this will almost build itself, and following the bouncing ball is going to keep you organised for life. Having your financial house in order is now your 'new normal'.

The way to make a start on your Bulletproof Checklist is to examine each of the rooms of your financial house and ask what needs tidying up. If you refer to the success statements that you developed last chapter as part of your Report Card, it doesn't take much imagination to start coming up with clear action items that would find a good home in the Bulletproof Checklist.

You tick these tasks off once done and repeat them next cycle when that particular checkpoint is due for review. As you start to gain more experience with the Method, that list develops and grows.

Phone a friend?

There's a shortcut to this process: ask an expert. Imagine asking the questions above of an independent expert who can get their head around what it is you're trying to achieve and apply their tech-savvy experience to your particular objective. Imagine the gold nuggets they'd give you to add to your Checklist.

It's worth doing, and so next chapter I'm going to give you some tips on the qualities this person needs to have.

Okay, you've rounded the final turn and you're now headed for the finish line.

Ah ha's . . .

- *The IP4R Method is all about delivering you results, time after time after time, with all the reliability of a Swiss watch. Progress meetings are a key touchpoint designed for you to check in on your progress towards those results.*
- *The agendas for your progress meetings ensure nothing is missed and that important questions are asked to confirm (a) that the strategies you're employing are still ideal, and (b) that all possible hurdles and potential obstacles have been considered.*
- *As you roll out the Independent Planning-for-results Method, you will progressively build your Optimise-to-Bulletproof Checklist, that task list which keeps your Financial House in perfect order for good.*

Conclusions & Resources

Where will you be this time next month?

Making your results braggable.

What to Do Next

"The way to get started is to quit talking and start doing."
—Walt Disney

Where are you now, and, if you made a start today, where could you be this time next month? What would that mean to your sense of certainty, your clarity about your current reality, and your confidence about your family's future?

From confidence to inevitability

At this point in the book, it's more likely you're impressed and excited by all this thinking and doing that goes into fortifying your finances and your objectives, than sceptical.

However, it's not beyond the realms of possibility that a fleeting thought might have wandered through your head along the lines of: "*I wonder whether this is all a bit much?*"

If that did happen to you, frankly I'm gratified, because you're starting to get it.

Years of work, years of trial and error, years of tinkering and perfecting, and the sweat of many, many brows went into what you now have in your hands as a finished, functional machine. We, the undersigned, are *dead serious* about you having a method that gives you *certainty*.

The question is: are you?

You've identified financial objectives for you and your family that are not mere goals, these are the 'must-haves' of your future. Holding these must-haves in your hands, you go out into a world full of uncertainty and danger.

It's a minefield out there.

And when you wander out into a minefield, you don't

recover easily from mistakes. You've got one shot at it: poor navigation decisions, taking directions from the wrong person, putting your foot in the wrong place—these have dire consequences. At the expense of sounding melodramatic, the 'Minefield of Finance' works very similarly.

The IP4R Method exists to help you navigate your way through the minefield without blowing up from a poor choice. Because this is so very true, Plan B Reviews are a critical component of bulletproof finances.

The more you do them, the better you get at them, the more you and your family will benefit.

As we near the end of our journey together, there is perhaps one final signpost to watch for on your road to optimising your finances and bulletproofing your future.

Success is easier with a team

I've spoken several times during the course of this book about having a team. No, you aren't doomed to fail without one. But it's easier with one. A team, that is.

> *"What could we accomplish if we knew*
> *we could not fail?"*
>
> **—Eleanor Roosevelt**

There's no getting around it, you stand to benefit from the input of professionals in certain areas—you can't do brain surgery yourself but you can become informed and get yourself into a state of organisation so you're going to enhance the prospects of your brain surgeon doing a superlative job. Make it easy for the surgeon—you're the beneficiary!

But that's just specialist advice. I'm talking about having a team behind you.

I've had the good fortune to meet a number of individuals who accomplished very significant achievements in their lives, in various walks of life from sport, to arts, to politics. One thing I found in common with all their stories was that (a) they were **very** serious about achieving their aim, and (b) they had a **team** behind them who was focussed on the same aim.

Why would your ambition to make your family's future absolutely bulletproof be any less worthy an aim? Why should it be treated with any less seriousness?

The well-being and future success of your family—your children and your partner—is at least as important, I suggest, as the achievements of sportspeople, artists, or any other high achiever you care to mention. Why, then, would you give this anything less than the best possible chances of success?

Look at it this way . . .

We've all heard about the studies that show 'accountability' positively impacts consistent results. What this means is that having someone you trust hold you accountable is more effective than flying solo. Like me, I'm sure you've had the experience of promising to yourself you'd get up way, way early tomorrow morning for a brisk walk, run, or workout . . . only to hit the snooze button. But, if I know there's someone waiting for me in the park so we can do the work together, you can take this to the bank: I'll be there.

Having a team aligned around a shared purpose takes a lot of the load off your shoulders and gives you a much higher probability of supremely improved results.

Who you need on your team

The IP4R Method puts you in the driver's seat and empowers you to take charge of your financial future. It isn't intended or capable of making you a qualified accountant, investment adviser or insurance expert. At some point, you're going to have to tap into those smarts to get the good oil. But not at the price of handing them the wheel. You're still captain of this ship and it's your job to get it to shore. There are those who'd prefer to keep you at sea, where you're forced to rely on them. This methodology ensures they are playing the role they are qualified, responsible enough paid to play, and no other. Certainly not yours.

However there's no shaking this—you are going to need input in some areas of your finances from an independent expert in that particular subject. We call these individuals 'Subject Matter Experts' or SMEs for short.

Who do you need on your team? Don't pick soldiers, pick Generals, they can worry about the soldiers. You need five Generals, one for each room in your financial house.

Cash planning	This General is primarily responsible for sourcing and coordinating all the advice you will need in cashflow, credit and finance, investments and social security. It's likely this individual will have expertise in at least one of these areas, but they will need to be sufficiently well connected to source the soldiers your army will need from their network to attend to all these disparate parts of cash planning.
Wealth planning	Your wealth planning General will ensure the quality and efficacy of all your planning needs that relate to the goal funding, financial modelling and investment analysis that's involved in this field.
Tax planning	This General will probably be an accountant who can supervise and coordinate all the tax, accounting and structuring needs you have in this planning department. He or she will have access to resources to get soldiers on board as they are needed and oversee their deployment.

Legal planning	Your General of legal planning is also most likely a lawyer who's a generalist but possibly a specialty in the sub-field of estate planning. This subject also demands access to a wide range of other legal specialisations crossing over into areas of business, investment, litigation, asset protection, and so on.
Risk planning	Risk planning is as broad a field as the law. Your General in this department will have a particular interest in risk management (especially the Plan B Review exercise), and contacts in the general insurance and life underwriting areas.

The expertise of your SMEs will likely cross over into other fields here and there, and some of your SMEs will wear multiple hats from time to time. The main thing to remember is the reason they're on your team: to help you get your Financial House in bulletproof order and keep it that way, for the benefit of you and your family, now and forever.

There might seem like perfectly legitimate reasons for soldiering on solo. If you had any hesitation whatever to the suggestion of enlisting help in this quest, then maybe you've thought:

Getting help is going to cost money.

It's time consuming.

To do it I'd have to expose myself.

I really don't want to have to go through all this with someone else.

I don't even know what I'd say to them or what help to ask for.

I don't know who to trust.

I don't know if they're any good.

Getting the help of a highly competent, experienced and professional team is only something you'd decline to do if you hadn't yet met anyone who fits this description or you genuinely believe you can do a better job in your spare time. On the other hand, getting help frees you up to enjoy life.

Think of it this way . . . the key to a healthy, long-lived life has a lot to do with activities entirely within your control: your nutrition, your exercise, proper rest and recuperation, regular relief from stress, good relationships with people you care about, meaning in your professional life, and so on. But when you catch something nasty, break your leg skiing, or your genetics let you down . . . you're going to need something extra.

It's at that point you need to consult someone with expertise in that particular area. And so too with your finances. It might mean buying an insurance policy, or choosing a retirement fund to invest in, or executing a trust document. You get the idea.

Lacking that connection to someone in this space is not a reason not to get started. You can make an enormous amount of planning and executing progress without that particular expert. So when it comes time to get one, you'll find one.

This Method leaves nothing to chance and is unparalleled anywhere. There's nothing like it. Will you, a year from now, wish you had started today?

Beyond Bulletproof

Taking that one step further, what happens after you have followed this Method to get your entire Financial House in order?

The reality is that, once you've accomplished a state of bulletproof certainty in your future finances, there is another challenge waiting for you: what to do with your freed-up energy and time. Life is for living and there are certain things you can't delegate.

How will you spend your time now that you're not bogged down with worries about your family's future? The truth is that your team will be doing a much better job than you ever did, attending to the minutiae of your financial affairs. So what are you going to do with your time?

If you follow the Method I've outlined in this book, then most likely within the next 12 to 18 months you're going to be 'certified financially organised' and feel much clearer and more certain about your family's future. So this question I'm asking is not a question about an impossibly unlikely event, like "*What am I going to do once I've won the lottery?*" . . . this is something that is most assuredly going to be your next challenge. I've seen it many times.

As a matter of fact, it most commonly arises as a struggle for recently retired folks. You see, their entire identity has been caught up for the last 40 years or more in being productive, creating business, bringing home the bacon, and solving big problems. And now that's all over.

You know the most common reaction? Grief. Yep, a sense of loss and a process of mourning that loss. Recovering from that to reconnect with other long-dormant aspects of the marrow of life . . . it's a time-costly process that, frankly, doesn't need to be that way. You can start preparing for your new appreciation for life today.

To show you what I mean by this, consider how Edmund Hillary, the conqueror of Mt Everest, felt when it finally dawned on him that he was too old to climb mountains anymore. He'd spent his entire life doing impossible things. It's fair to say he was reasonably invested in this identity. And suddenly it was gone. How did he deal with this?

> *"When I was 50 years old, I actually decided to draw up a list of half a dozen things that I really hadn't done very well, and I was going to make efforts to improve."*

As impossible as it might be to believe, he was a lousy skier. This is a guy who trekked through the snow all the way to the South Pole.

> *"One of them was skiing, and I really did become a very much better skier."*

What about you? There are musical instruments to learn, relationships to nurture, new skills to acquire, other languages to speak, books on the shelf you've never had time to enjoy, qualifications you've always wanted, places to visit, people to meet and stories to tell, maybe even your own.

Life is calling to you. With this in mind, let's consider what to do next.

Next steps

We've nearly reached the end of our time together, my dear reader. I sincerely hope that you've benefited in more ways than one.

Within the pages of this book, you have a Method that you can use to cut through the complexity and dangers of this money minefield and make the future you really want a certain reality. My greatest hope in writing this book is that it has helped inspire you to go ahead and do that.

With that in mind, let's take one last look over our shoulder at where we've come from so you can decide what you're going to do with all this information.

In the first few chapters of this book, we took an in-depth examination of your current situation.

We looked at what was bothering you enough for you to pick up this book in the first place, as well as some realities of 'the human condition' that were contributing to your stalemate with progress. Some self-assessments helped light the way

Next, we looked at how getting financially organised — the key component to **The Independent Planning-for-results Method** — is a sure way to break through your glass ceiling and bulletproof your finances to create a more certain future.

The concept of your Financial House was introduced to break down the complexity of your financial life into bite-sized chunks, making it simpler and easier to organise. We also took a look at the challenges and hurdles that are part of this approach. By now it is clear just what is within your power to solve your worries, frustrations and challenges.

In the next big chapter of this book, we explored the three phases you follow when executing this method.

We explored a number of valuable intellectual property assets you create as you execute the process, assets that get you on track and keep you there, to progressively replace anxiety with certainty, with transparency.

Next we unpacked the core concepts essential to making good progress with this Method.

You stepped through exercises that give you a strong start, with examples along the way. You saw how to define success in each 'room' of your Financial House and measure your progress along the way to your Must-Haves, as well as progress to bulletproof certainty in your financial future.

Along the way we explained what skills you could pick up to support your efforts and some exceptionally valuable assets that you would use to make failure all but impossible.

Last of all, we turned to the value of a team in your quest, plus who you need to be part of your team, and the skills and connections they need to possess.

The reasons for a team were examined, both from the point of view of turbo boosting your progress, but also to make it easier for you to turn your attention to more important aspects of life than having your finances dominate your attention.

Because the reality is another challenge awaits you beyond your pending achievement of becoming financially organised, and it would be better if you start preparing for that now.

This point is probably as good a place as any to wind up our time together because not only does it bring us up to date with where we're at, it's also a neat segue to summarise what I'm really trying to teach you here in this entire book . . .

It is not the mountain that we conquer, but ourselves.

—Edmund Hillary

My message-in-a-bottle to you

When you have justified reasons to feel confident about your finances and optimistic about your future, it's no longer necessary for you to white-knuckle the steering wheel. When you feel relaxed enough to do that, you can start to enjoy the scenery out the window.

This framework you now have is actually designed with the purpose of getting your finance worries out of your face so you can focus on enjoying the experience of life. It's hard to see a beautiful sunset with your problems in your face. The sunset won't be there forever, and if you lock yourself into these problems, you might miss it.

There is another option. But really getting your head around this alternative starts with realising something very simple yet profound . . .

The hand in your face obscuring your view and preventing you from seeing the view is yours.

The moment you realise this is the moment you can breathe a sigh of relief, relax your arm and let your hand drop away from your face, revealing the beauty of the sunset that was behind it.

Don't worry, your hand is still there, attached to your arm. It just doesn't need to be in your face anymore.

Instead, place your hand in the hand of someone who's offering theirs. This Method is me offering my hand to you.

What's your next step? My friend, **start**.

Sure, decide if you want help or if you want to go it alone, but start. Make one small decision, then take that first step and experience that exquisite lightness-of-being that comes with the knowledge that you have just turned your ship around to face your port-of-dreams.

I sincerely congratulate you on having completed your journey with me through this book and—from the bottom of my heart—I wish you and yours my very, very—**very**—best.

Sincerely,

Dan.

How to Get More Help

"It always seems impossible until it's done."
—Nelson Mandela

In this book you have in your hands everything you need for you to accomplish the same results that this Method continues to deliver for many, many other families. And then some.

It's no word of a lie to say that I've absolutely 'given away the farm' to you in this book. All of the incredible power of this Method, having evolved over several decades of trial and error, is now yours to wield for the benefit of you and your family.

But that doesn't mean you shouldn't ask for help if you want it.

In the link you received when you purchased this book I've included some additional resources for you, partly as "*congratulations for reading this book*" and partly as "*I didn't have enough room in the book but I still want to teach it to you.*" The links below will take you to privately hosted materials where you can access the additional training.

Also, I've included information and a link on how my team and I can help you with every step of The Independent Planning-for-results Method. We have multiple offerings, from DIY digital courses to full service done-for-you options.

Book Bonus 1

"Swimming with Sharks audiobook", 4-hour audio recording of the book, read by the author.

Book Bonus 2

"Swimming with Sharks companion workbook." Companion manual for the book, with coaching notes on completing templates plus 8 examples of completed templates. Included are all the templates and example exercises gathered together in one workbook, with step-by-step instructions on completing the templates plus extra notes and tips from the author.

Work with a team to accelerate your results

My team and I—we live and breathe this stuff and we're genuinely excited at the prospect of another joining the ranks of those who are financially organised and experiencing the life they and their family deserve. Don't wait, give us a call for a chat because we want to help:

www.danielbrammall.com/roadmap-page

About the Author

"Everyone knew it was impossible,
until a fool who didn't know
came along and did it."

—Albert Einstein

Born in New York but having lived almost his whole life in Australia, Daniel Brammall's been a financial adviser his entire career.

His introduction to the harsh environment of the finance industry was at the tender age of 22 where he, as a university graduate, earned his stripes pounding the pavement selling life insurance door-to-door.

Inspired by a thirst for knowledge and the heartfelt desire to be part of a profession he could be proud of, in 2009 he founded the Profession of Independent Financial Advisers (www.pifa.org.au).

Now in his fourth decade in finance, Daniel's accumulated a rich bank of experience but still maintains that "*the older I get, the more I realize how little I really know.*"

Today he spends much of his time advocating for a recognised profession in financial planning, coaching financial advisers on delivering conflict-free advice, and appears regularly in mainstream television and print media.

Two mantras guide his work ethic:

- from his experience in business . . . *"My value is set by the value I create for others,"* and
- from his twenty-something years as a black belt martial arts instructor . . . *"You're only as good as your last training session."*

All inquiries for speaking appearances can be sent to

admin@danielbrammall.com

Made in the USA
Monee, IL
11 November 2026

91e3d72c-ccea-4aff-b521-2aaa6d5f10f6R01